M000286140

HABITAT

ECOLOGY THINKING IN ARCHITECTURE

HABITAT

ECOLOGY THINKING IN ARCHITECTURE

Dirk van den Heuvel
Janno Martens
Víctor Muñoz Sanz
(eds.)

nai010 publishers

Contents

PREFACE

Guus Beumer

Telling stories, forgotten stories, or even better, uncovering new stories based on the materials in the vast collection of Het Nieuwe Instituut is one of the incentives behind the research programme of our institute, and our collaborations with Delft University of Technology and other parties.

The Jaap Bakema Study Centre, the research initiative established between Delft University of Technology and Het Nieuwe Instituut, has set itself the task to bring out such narratives, to throw a questioning light on accepted histories, as well as to reveal surprising insights or deliberately ignored perspectives and demonstrate hitherto overlooked connections. *Habitat: Ecology Thinking in Architecture* builds on an exhibition held in 2018-2019, linked to the long-term research project Total Space. It occasioned various lectures, seminars and archive talks with students, architects and some of the historical protagonists.

This publication deploys the classic, modernist notion of habitat to probe the holdings of Het Nieuwe Instituut and at the same time to tell a story about hidden strands of ecological thinking in architecture that can be retraced between the various archives and files as collected by our institute. In light of the global environmental crisis of today, ecology is urgent as a topic and can simply no longer be ignored or marginalized to the fringes of architecture. A search in the collection immediately reveals a multiplicity of beginnings and positions on the matter, and in such a way that is has expanded far beyond the historical borders of a disciplinary definition of both architecture and ecology. Public presentations and research projects from our institute all depart from such expansive ecology thinking: for instance, last year's Neuhaus, a temporary academy for more-than-human knowledge, the ongoing nursing of our New Garden, and the Dutch national presentation Multispecies Urbanism at the 17th Venice Architecture Biennale, scheduled for 2021.

Habitat: Ecology Thinking in Architecture revisits authoritative sources, such as the CIAM discourse and the Team 10 meetings from the post-war period, while combining these with other positions and events, among those the largely unknown, yet influential work of Pjotr Gonggrijp, whose analytical maps of the Dutch delta gained a veritable cult status in the 1970s. The legacy of ecological activist Joost Váhl holds a similar position and together with the history of the seemingly everyday, suburban district of Tanthof in Delft, actually marks a break in thinking about the interrelations between the Dutch (man-made) polder landscape, ecology, architecture and planning.

In the combination of well-known and unheard voices, brought together through the lens of ecology, lies a key for other stories, for unexpected moments of imagination, of multiplicity, of architecture or design in general as activist engagement. I can only hope that these combinations lead to a shared idea of urgency and an openness towards these longer lines of thought that have often been ignored. This will not only contribute to our insights in what has been thought, developed, cherished and in some cases again forgotten, it will also contribute to the further development of the specific composition of archives in the national collection.

Eventually, ecology thinking goes far beyond the confines of the discipline of architecture and its institutionalized memory, which is not only selective – in terms of those all too familiar categories of nationality, gender, race, class and so forth – but it is also so terribly slow for the impatient activist! To the curator and the archivist a collection presents an ecology of its own, whereas ecology thinking also implies the politics of diversity and inclusion as a matter of course. Ecology thinking implies growth and change – as the architects of the CIAM and Team 10 had to admit and incorporate into their reconceptualization of the discipline.

Ecology thinking involves empathy, and the recognition of the multiple stories that are out there. We are in urgent need of all those strands in order to weave a critical and productive narrative on the historical relation between architecture and ecology.

Dirk van den Heuvel

HABITAT AND ARCHITECTURE
Disruption and Expansion

Cover of the proceedings of CIAM 10, 1956

Alison Smithson, future chronicler of Team 10, at the Dubrovnik CIAM congress, 1956, photograph by John Voelcker

1   Alison and Peter Smithson, comments as part of 'Thoughts in Progress: The New Brutalism', *Architectural Design* (April 1957), 113.

2   Besides the National Collection at Het Nieuwe Instituut in Rotterdam, other architecture archives that hold CIAM materials include the GTA institute ETH Zurich and the Special Collections at GSD Harvard University.

3   For an overview of the history of the CIAM see: Eric Mumford, *The CIAM Discourse on Urbanism, 1928-1960* (Cambridge, MA: MIT Press, 2000). For the post-war period see the special issue of *Rassegna* (December 1992), 'The Last CIAMs', compiled by Jos Bosman.

4   Archive of Cornelis van Eesteren, Collection Het Nieuwe Instituut (EEST_4.200). Copies of these proceedings are also in other CIAM archives, including the ETH Zurich and GSD Harvard University.

A Disruptive Term

Habitat was not always a central concept in architecture. As a specialist term from biology, anthropology and social geography, it has a life and history of its own outside architecture. When it was appropriated by architects in the mid-twentieth century, it was a source of inspiration and innovation, yet also caused strife and upheaval. As such, the term habitat has been disruptive to architecture. This might be surprising, since the two seem naturally and closely related. After all, the term stems from the Latin *habitare*, or to dwell. And architecture provides houses and housing.

Ecology has become most popular in reconceptualizing not only architecture, but our whole way of being in the world, due to such provocative thinkers as Gilles Deleuze and Felix Guattari, and Donna Haraway. The aim of this book is not an exercise in theory, however, but to present a close reading of recent architecture history to positions of today. It does so by a selection from various archives that aims to identify a burgeoning ecology thinking in architecture and planning, and its impact on current ideas.

So how could habitat be disruptive to architecture? Why and how exactly? And what came out of this disruption that might be of interest today?

A Larger Whole

When the term was introduced in architecture in the circles of the CIAM, the renowned *Congrès Internationaux d'Architecture Moderne*, it became a hotly debated and contested topic. It was the aftermath of the Second World War. In Europe, architects and planners put all their energy in the reconstruction of cities and their new expansions, into modernizing national economies and literally building the new post-war, collective welfare arrangements – either in the liberal democracies in the West, the autocratic regimes on the Iberic peninsula, or state communism in the East.

Besides rethinking the urgent housing question, the notion of habitat brought a profoundly new way of conceiving architecture and planning. No longer could one consider buildings and cities as discrete, isolated objects, instead they were to be understood as part of a larger whole, an environment or indeed a habitat. Architecture was no longer a discipline of autonomy, but something relational, embedded, conditional as well as contextual. To think of architecture in terms of habitat set off a shift from a world of pure form towards a social pattern.

Architectural values of permanence and durability were combined with, or made way for, those of growth and change. Habitat as a central concept in architecture brought a change from architecture as an abstract, intellectual construct to a practice of working intuitively with the raw situation and matter at hand, to 'drag a rough poetry out of the confused and powerful forces which are at work' as the proponents of New Brutalism, Alison and Peter Smithson, stated in 1957.[1]

Not for Publication

The archives of the National Collection for Dutch Architecture and Urbanism hold numerous dossiers that document the discussions on modern architecture within the CIAM.[2] Set up in 1928 with the sponsorship of Hélène de Mandrot, patron of the arts and an artist herself, the CIAM was to become one of the most influential international architects' associations to promote the cause of modern architecture. Twenty-four architects from eight countries came together in La Sarraz to sign its foundational declaration, among whom such illustrious but also very different characters as Hendrik Berlage, Gerrit Rietveld, Ernst May, Hugo Häring, André Lurçat, Gabriel Guévrékian, and perhaps most notably, Sigfried Giedion and Le Corbusier, who would be among the leading voices of the new organization.[3]

The CIAM soon developed into what we now might call a platform for architectural design research in response to the issue of large-scale urbanization and industrialization, and their concomitant social problems. While most of these archival documents are solely interesting for specialists, they also hold the key to start unpacking the history of our cities and buildings, and how they are theorized and conceived. One such document is the proceedings of the tenth CIAM congress, held in Dubrovnik in 1956.[4] Its dark-blue cover holds a clear message: 'not for publication', a gesture of censorship that seems contradictory to the spirit of the CIAM, whose leading figures were such eloquent masters in propagating their ideas.

The compiled contents are basically a report of the discussions on the issue of habitat, the main topic of the congress. In those years, the CIAM had assigned itself to formulate a so-called Charter of Habitat, in order to clarify the necessary future direction of architecture and planning, especially in the field of housing. However, despite earlier attempts, the congress ended without a shared ambition that could be translated into a proper Charter. There would be no official synthesizing document on the particular topic of habitat. The historical proceedings are a testimony of discord and internal criticism, a clash of ideas and minds.

Dirk van den Heuvel

Agonistics and Knowledge Production

Despite the CIAM's failure to produce a clearly formulated Charter of Habitat, its legacy has turned out to be a rich body for continuous historical and theoretical research. It is exactly because of the belligerent and agonistic quality of the debates, on habitat among other things, that the CIAM legacy lends itself as such productive research material with a special role for the surviving archival documents. As becomes clear from past and ongoing research, the body of historical documents demonstrates how the CIAM was not simply a platform for the promotion of a clear-cut, unified ideology, but rather how the association of architects created an arena for exchange between peers, and clearly, for dispute and strife, too.

Today, the notion of agonistics is popular through the writings of Chantal Mouffe, who situates it in the political realm, stating it is part and parcel of the democratic process.[5] Before her, Johan Huizinga noted in *Homo Ludens* that human knowledge production is polemical and agonistic by nature, and that the validity of propositions is tested through controversy and competition.[6] Both Mouffe and Huizinga – coming from very different disciplines – also state that a certain assigned space is needed to have these agonistics play out. It is one more reason why the CIAM organization is a fertile test bed to architecture researchers: again, not as a unified body of thought, but as the dynamic of propositions and interactions, through which architectural knowledge and values were produced, and eventually operationalized.

Such an understanding of the CIAM as an arena of agonistic knowledge production enables researchers to open up its received histories, and to move beyond the canonical readings, while bringing out overlooked and suppressed voices. Building on these observations and making new selections, one is able to point out continuities and shifting positions. It allows for new insights in the interconnections and branches of a network of ideas and people, through which and who the development of architectural knowledge can be mapped and held to light. The epistemological issues at stake can be foregrounded, in this case the one of habitat as ecology thinking, including the involved interdisciplinary traffic.

From the Functional City to Habitat

From the history of the post-war CIAM events it becomes clear it was Le Corbusier himself who announced the new focus on habitat. In 1949, at the seventh CIAM congress in Bergamo, Le Corbusier declared that the CIAM should work towards a Charter of Habitat without much further explanation.[7] Little did he know that the introduction of the topic of habitat heralded the demise of the CIAM, just ten years later at its last congregation in Otterlo in 1959.

Clearly, Le Corbusier viewed such a Charter of Habitat as an elaboration of the famous Charter of Athens, which he himself had helped to formulate in the summer of 1933. Then already Le Corbusier had likened urban planning to a 'biology of the world'.[8] The Athens Charter summed up the CIAM's ambitions for modern architecture and city planning. It was delivered during one of those myth-making moments in the history of modern architecture: the cruise on board of the SS *Patris II* between Marseilles and Athens, which had accommodated the fourth CIAM congress.[9]

5 Chantal Mouffe, *Agonistics: Thinking the World Politically* (London: Verso, 2013); Ernesto Laclau and Chantal Mouffe, *Hegemony and Socialist Strategy: Towards a Radical Democratic Politics* (London: Verso, 1985).
6 Johan Huizinga, *Homo Ludens: A Study of the Play-Element in Culture* (London/Boston/Henley: Routledge/Kegan Paul, 1949, 1980), 133 and 156, originally published in Dutch as: *Homo Ludens: Proeve eener bepaling van het spel-element der cultuur* (Haarlem, 1938). For a discussion of the relevance of *Homo Ludens* to the Team 10 discourse, see: Dirk van den Heuvel, 'Team 10 Riddles: A Few Notes on Mythopoiesis, Discourse and Epistemology', in: Max Risselada, Dirk van den Heuvel and Gijs de Waal (eds.), *Team 10: Keeping the Language of Modern Architecture Alive* (Delft: TU Delft, 2006), 89-108.

7 Mumford, *The CIAM Discourse on Urbanism*, op. cit. (note 3), 187.
8 Ibid., 79.
9 Evelien van Es et al. (eds.), *Atlas of the Functional City: CIAM 4 and Comparative Urban Analysis* (Bussum: Thoth, 2014).
10 Mumford, *The CIAM Discourse on Urbanism*, op. cit. (note 3), 192.
11 See the essay by Leonardo Zuccaro Marchi, 'Between *Habiter* and Habitat: CIAM and the Sigtuna Meeting 1952', on pages 26-33 of this publication.
12 These projects have been intensely studied and still figure prominently in post-colonial studies in architecture. Jean-Louis Cohen, Monique Eleb and Zeynep Çelik's groundbreaking work should be mentioned here, just as the writings of Tom Avermaete, Marion von Osten and Maristella Casciato.

13 Annie Pedret, in: 'CIAM IX: Discussing the Charter of Habitat', in: Max Risselada and Dirk van den Heuvel (eds.), *Team 10: In Search of a Utopia of the Present* (Rotterdam: NAi Publishers, 2005), 21.
14 Mumford, *The CIAM Discourse on Urbanism*, op. cit. (note 3), 248.
15 For the history of Team 10, see: Risselada and Van den Heuvel, *Team 10*, op. cit. (note 13); Annie Pedret, *Team 10: An Archival History* (London/New York: Routledge, 2013).
16 The Manifesto was the outcome of an unofficial meeting signed by the Team 10 members Jaap Bakema, Aldo van Eyck, Daniel van Ginkel, Hans Hovens Greve Peter Smithson and John Voelcker.

17 Bakema's films are in the National Collection for Dutch Architecture and Urban Planning at Het Nieuwe Instituut, Rotterdam.
18 The congress report was published by Jürgen Joedicke for Karl Krämer Verlag: Oscar Newman (ed.), *CIAM '59 in Otterlo* (Stuttgart: Karl Krämer Verlag, 1961).

The Athens Charter enshrined the concept of the Functional City as one of the CIAM's main tenets, along with the minimum dwelling and rational land subdivision. Central dogma of the Functional City idea was the separation of urban functions by zoning, with the four categories of dwelling, work, recreation and transport as the four main functions. At the Bergamo conference, most energy was dedicated to furthering the ambitions of the Athens Charter, with meetings devoted to 'Putting the Athens Charter into Practice', and a plenary session on 'Applications of the Athens Charter'.[10]

So perhaps unsurprisingly, after its first mention by Le Corbusier, habitat didn't immediately take centre-stage in the CIAM discourse. The next CIAM congress in Hoddesdon in 1951 was devoted to the theme of 'The Heart of the City' and the issues of modern monumentality, civic values and public space. But at the following intermediate CIAM meeting in Sigtuna in 1952, the topic of habitat returned with a vengeance. A dispute ensued over its exact definition and scope, most stingingly between two of Le Corbusier's protégés, André Wogenscky and Georges Candilis. Broadly speaking, the debates moved between the poles of habitat as limited to the question of housing, and habitat as a holistic, socioecological approach to urbanism.[11]

Yet, more importantly with regard to the future of the CIAM, the notion of habitat was deployed against the doctrine of the Functional City and its rationalist, analytic approach to architecture and city building. For the critics of Functionalism, habitat seemed to offer the possibility to redeem the CIAM and modern architecture, to save it from technocracy and to move beyond the Functional City of zoning and separation. Instead of offering the possibility of synthesis and common purpose for the CIAM, habitat became a subject of contestation and internal critique with regard to the future direction of modern architecture.

The Emergence of Team 10

Enthusiasm for habitat peaked at the CIAM congress in Aix-en-Provence in 1953. This was largely due to the presentations of the groups from Morocco and Algeria: GAMMA (Groupe d'architectes modernes Marocains) and CIAM-Alger. Building on French colonial planning practices, these presentations brought a new perspective on local dwelling practices through their focus on the *bidonvilles* of Casablanca and Algiers, the poor, informal settlements of rural workers who had migrated to the city.[12] Also, the project for Alexanderpolder, a new town east of Rotterdam by the Dutch CIAM group Opbouw received much acclaim

for its attempt to arrive at a project of integration of functions, rather than separation.[13] Yet despite the success of the congress, an overwhelming attendance of close to 3,000 architects, and a festive party on the roof terrace of Le Corbusier's recently finished Unité d'Habitation apartment building, the congress ended indecisively.

Conventionally, the post-war CIAM congresses and their unfolding have been portrayed as a generation conflict. For the first time, the congress of 1953 saw the official participation of so-called younger members, who had joined the various national delegations. The protagonists themselves, too, often used it as an explanation for the course of events. Le Corbusier set the tone, once again, when he declared it was time for the 'generation of 1928' to make room for a new generation, the 'First-CIAM' had to pass on the baton to the 'Second-CIAM'.[14]

Some of the most engaged younger members organized themselves in Team 10, a group of a shifting composition with a couple of core members as leading voices, in particular Jaap Bakema, Georges Candilis, Aldo van Eyck, Alison and Peter Smithson, and Shadrach Woods, later joined by Giancarlo de Carlo.[15] Ahead of the formation of Team 10, some of them produced the Statement on Habitat of 1954, also known as the Doorn Manifesto.[16] In hindsight it is often seen as one of the founding documents of Team 10. The same year Team 10 was made responsible for another attempt to arrive at a Charter of Habitat, and was assigned with the preparations for the tenth CIAM congress. It was initially planned for Algiers in 1955, but partly due to the start of the Algerian war of independence it was eventually convened in Dubrovnik in 1956.

Bakema brought his 16mm film camera along. The images convey an atmosphere of summery bliss.[17] Shots of swimming in the Adriatic Sea and socializing on terraces are mixed with impressions of the working meetings at the Museum of Modern Art just outside the fortifications of the old town. But such paradisiacal context was to no avail. The CIAM's resolution to deliver a Charter of Habitat was not fulfilled. It was decided that the national CIAM delegations would abolish themselves for a more flexible organization of kindred spirits. Three years later, at the Otterlo congress organized by Bakema, the whole organization of the CIAM was disbanded.[18] Team 10 continued to meet until 1981 and the notion of habitat would haunt its exchanges.

Knowledge Transfers

The CIAM itself was very much aware of the importance of knowledge production, its documentation and

**Opbouw, Rotterdam,
presentation grid of Pendrecht
district, for CIAM 7 in Bergamo,
1949**

**Jaap Bakema and Peter
Smithson, CIAM 10 in Dubrovnik
1956**

19   Alison Smithson (ed.), *Team
10 Meetings 1953-1984* (New York:
Rizzoli, 1991), 14, see also note 31
on the same page.
20   The newsletters (18 in total)
are kept at Het Nieuwe Instituut
(BAKE.1_10301019).
21   Annie Pedret extensively
studied the debates on the CIAM
grid in her 2001 dissertation; see also
Annie Pedret, 'Dismantling the
CIAM Grid: New Values for Modern
Architecture', in: Risselada and
Van den Heuvel, *Team 10*, op. cit.
(note 13), 252-257; Pedret, *Team 10*,
op. cit. (note 15), 58-61 and 94-96.
22   'Preparation for CIAM X',
dated December 1955, Bakema
archive, Het Nieuwe Instituut
(BAKE_0155).

23   Catherine Blain (ed.), *L'Atelier
de Montrouge: La modernité à
l'oeuvre 1958-1981* (Paris: Actes
Sud, Cité de l'Architecture et du
Patrimoine, 2008).
24   Monika Platzer published
the contributions by the Austrian
CIAM: *Cold War and Architecture:
The Competing Forces that Reshaped
Austria after 1945* (Zurich: Park
Books, 2020), 264-271. Marcela
Hanáčková is preparing a
dissertation on the Czechoslovakian
contribution: Marcela Hanáčková,
'Team 10 and Czechoslovakia:
Secondary Networks', in: Łukasz
Stanek (ed.), *Team 10 East:
Revisionist Architecture in Real
Existing Modernism* (Warsaw:
Museum of Modern Art, 2014),
73-99.
25   Both are included in this book,
on pages 36 and 78-81.

dissemination, albeit not in terms of agonistics or a polyphonic association. Team 10 would be much more conscious about creating such an arena for debate. Alison Smithson described her reports of the Team 10 meetings as allowing the different voices to speak for themselves, to 'start different trains of thought in different readers'.[19] Yet, her account has also been fiercely criticized for being biased, or at least too selective, by both other Team 10 members and historians. After the last CIAM congress in Otterlo, Jaap Bakema opened up a 'Post Box for the Development of Habitat', a newsletter that was compiled by himself from the many letters and submissions he received, and circulated around the world to friends and colleagues through his office.[20] While personally curated, the newsletter was also a polyphonic organ with contributions by notable authors, including Fumihiko Maki, Oskar Hansen and Yona Friedman. Rather than synthesizing habitat thinking, it allowed for further expansion.

Such self-awareness was partially the reason for the development of the so-called CIAM grid, to present the research design projects. The Grille CIAM d'Urbanisme was developed by the French CIAM group ASCORAL (Assemblée de constructeurs pour une Rénovation architecturale). Basically, the grid was nothing but a set of presentation panels with all the information organized according to graphic rules, and the specifics of defined categories, among which the four basic functions of the Functional City concept. The purpose was to objectify the various projects of the CIAM members, to be able to compare them and to isolate and synthesize key concepts and design tools. The CIAM grid as a cognitive instrument became a target of contestation too, however, quite like the Charter of Habitat.[21]

The ASCORAL grid was criticized for encouraging further separation and isolation of the many elements that constitute a modern city and collective life without offering effective synthesis. Moreover, at the CIAM congress in Aix, the many grids on display were incredibly lengthy. Therefore, for the tenth congress in Dubrovnik, Team 10 proposed to limit presentations to four panels. These had to contain a problem statement, a general and detailed design solution, and a statement of principles.[22] The energy should be aimed at creating coherence to address 'the whole problem of environment', as the Smithsons put it.

Both grids were in fact excellent research exchange facilitators, not only for the congress debates, but also to disseminate copies. For the Dubrovnik congress, participants were urged to hand in two formats: one large with colour for the congress presentations, and one small in black-and-white for future publications. Today, many but certainly not all,

survive in the archives as testimony to the CIAM and Team 10 exchanges.

Holes in the Archives

When broadening the historiographical scope beyond the received canon of the CIAM and Team 10, one of the immediate effects is the appearance of all sorts of holes and gaps in the various archival holdings. To focus on Dubrovnik 1956, the 'not for publication' proceedings mentions 35 contributions in total, many of which are missing from the archives.

The sizeable French contribution has been lost for instance, not only the one by the ASCORAL group, but also by the Groupe Cité from Paris, with Roger Aujame and the future members of the Atelier de Montrouge, Pierre Riboulet, Gérard Thurnauer and Jean-Louis Véret, contemporaries of Team 10 who worked in a similar spirit.[23] Also, the presentation grid of the Berlin Hansaviertel by Hubert Hoffman remains unknown, just like the one of the famous case of the Vällingby new town in Sweden. Presentations by The Planning Workshop from New York, or two housing projects from Israel remain an enigma.

Some grids were brought to light recently, such as the urban renewal project for the inner city of Vienna by Wilhelm Schütte, and the presentations from Czechoslovakia, which followed the architectural doctrine of Socialist Realism.[24] In the archives in Rotterdam the presentation from Philadelphia and one of the two Finnish presentations are kept. Both involved future Team 10 members, Blanche Lemco in the case of Philadelphia, and Reima Pietilä in the latter.[25]

Surprisingly, there was no contribution by Georges Candilis and Shadrach Woods, even when the two of them were present in Dubrovnik, and actively participated in the committee meetings. At the CIAM congress in Aix, their projects in Casablanca were one of the eye-catchers as part of the celebrated GAMMA presentation. Perhaps this omission was due to the fact they had just relocated from Morocco to Paris, and were not active in the French CIAM groups. Still, this is only speculation.

Sometimes one gets a glimpse, though. One of the rare photos of the Dubrovnik event shows Peter Smithson talking to the room. We see Jaqueline Tyrwhitt from behind, next to her a microphone for recording the conversations. Jaap Bakema looks at a note in his right hand. The project that Smithson is explaining is not his own though, it is the project for the famous Cluster Block apartment tower in Bethnal Green, London, designed by Denys Lasdun with Lindsay Drake and realized in 1957. The four panels on the mantelpiece have gone missing, and it

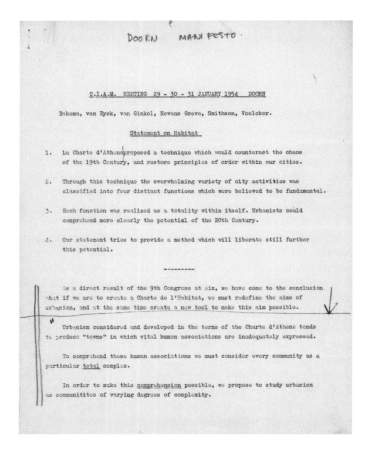

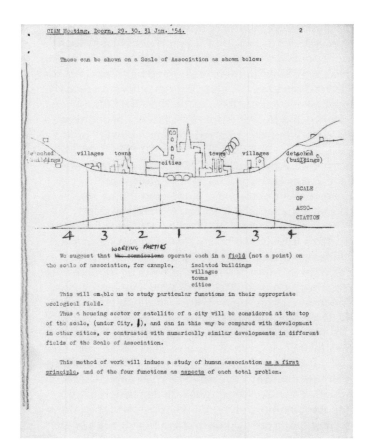

'Statement on Habitat' by Jaap Bakema, Aldo van Eyck, Daniel van Ginkel, Hans Hovens Greve, Peter Smithson, and John Voelcker, version Jaap Bakema, distributed 1 March 1954

26   The townhouses presentation can be found in this publication on page 43, and one of Voelcker's presentations is included on page 42. The proceedings also mention presentations by John Bicknell, Peter Ahrends and students from the AA school, but they seem to have gone missing.

27   The presentation is kept at the CCA; the rivalry between Stirling and the Smithsons has been noted by various authors. Stirling attended the Team 10 meeting at Royaumont in 1962, after which he was not invited anymore.

28   Kenneth Frampton, 'Souvenirs du Sous-développement', *l'Architecture d'Aujourd'hui* 344 (January-February 2003), 88-95.

29   Hadas Steiner, 'Life at the Threshold', *October* 136, New Brutalism (spring 2011), 133-155; Dean Hawkes, *Architecture and Climate: An Environmental History of British Architecture 1600-2000* (London/New York: Routledge, 2012).

30   Volker M. Welter, 'In-between Space and Society: On some British Roots of Team 10's Urban Thought in the 1950's', in: Risselada and Van den Heuvel, *Team 10*, op. cit. (note 13), 258-263. Geddes was a well-known reference in the British CIAM discourse, Jaqueline Tyrwhitt was most instrumental here, editing Geddes's writings and using his work in educational programmes she supervised, cf. Ellen Shoshkes, *Jaqueline Tyrwhitt: A Transnational Life in Urban Planning and Design* (London/New York: Routledge, 2016; Ashgate, 2013).

31   Letter from CIAM Nederland '8 + Opbouw', with the 'result of the intermediate meeting …at Doorn in Holland', Smithson papers, Het Nieuwe Instituut (TTEN_8).

32   Smithson, *Team 10 Meetings*, op. cit. (note 19), 68-69.

33   The Smithsons used various images from Gutkind's publications for their own, see Dirk van den Heuvel, *Alison and Peter Smithson: A Brutalist Story* (Delft: TU Delft, 2013), 199.

34   Jean-Louis Cohen, 'The Moroccan Group and the Theme of Habitat', *Rassegna* (December 1992), 58-67; Monique Eleb, 'An Alternative to Functionalist Universalism: Écochard, Candilis, and ATBAT-Afrique', in: Sarah Williams Goldhagen and Réjean Legault (eds.), *Anxious Modernisms: Experimentation in Postwar Architectural Culture* (Montréal/Cambridge MA: CCA/MIT Press, 2000), 55-73.

is only through this one photo that we see how Peter Smithson presented the various British presentations of the MARS group to the attendants. Among those contributions we also find the townhouses by Bill and Gillian Howell, John Killick and John Partridge, and two by John Voelcker.[26] Also interestingly, James Stirling had initially prepared a MARS contribution for a village extension, probably made for the pre-presentations in 1955 and eventually not presented in Dubrovnik.[27]

Team 10 and Ecology

In architecture, Team 10 is not immediately associated with ecology thinking, especially not since today ecological concepts are coupled with those of sustainability issues and climate change, which were non-existing topics at the time. Usually, the interrelations between social configurations and architecture are foregrounded in the various histories of Team 10. But the term is there, in the earliest drafts of the Statement on Habitat, just as it is in the writings of the Smithsons in particular. Kenneth Frampton is one of the few who has characterized the work of the Smithsons as 'proto-ecological'.[28] Hadas Steiner too, has discussed the ecological concepts present in the work of the Smithsons in relation to the topic of habitat, while others have pointed out the overlaps between their Brutalist work and a climate-responsive architecture.[29]

The Statement on Habitat of 1954 invited architects to think of their work as an intervention in an 'ecological field'. To explain such ecological fields, the document introduced Scottish biologist Patrick Geddes's Valley Section. As a diagram, the original Valley Section depicts a progression of human civilization from rural habitation to the modern metropolis.[30] For Team 10, it offered a tool to start understanding differences in context, density and complexity that called for different, particular architectural solutions rather than generic, rationalist formulas. Spanning an arc from isolate dwellings to hamlets and villages, to towns and cities, the Valley Section was translated into a 'scale of association'.[31] This interconnected scale of associations was to replace the doctrinaire separation of the four functions. The aspiration was to do justice to the specific context of local cultural identity, while also accommodating modernization.

Multiple Origins and Parallels

Habitat was to become a much used term in architecture and planning, and has been appropriated and promoted by various actors, from the Habitat policies for human settlements run by the UN since the 1970s, to the famous housing complex in Montréal of 1967, designed by Moshe Safdie. An early example comes from Lina Bo Bardi and her husband Pietro Bardi, who established the journal *Habitat* in 1950 shortly after having migrated to Brazil, to promote art and architecture in a combination of modernism with the vernacular and indigenous. Therefore, in terms of historiographical analysis, it is crucial to note that a genealogy of habitat in architecture consists of multiple origins and parallels.

When trying to map the many branches of habitat within the architecture discourse, one of the things to observe is that habitat was not only disruptive to architecture, it also resulted in expanding the discipline of architecture far beyond assumed certainties. Through the interdisciplinary traffic of concepts, mostly related to new principles of ordering, architecture was taken up in a most challenging exchange – between new theories of information and aesthetics, systems theory, biology and anthropology, the rise of computer science, but also linguistics. Thus, habitat as a disruptive term has also been transformative and transitional to architecture. Even from a relatively clearly demarcated domain as the circles of the CIAM and Team 10, a range of references springs up. One lucid instance from the Team 10 discourse remains the contribution by Christopher Alexander, who brought his research of an Indian village to the Team 10 meeting in Royaumont in 1962. From his survey he would translate the social and spatial relations into mathematical equations, the basis for his 1964 publication *Notes on the Synthesis of Form*.[32]

When contextualizing the ideas of the Smithsons, it is not only Patrick Geddes that comes to the fore. German architect and climate designer Otto Koenigsberger started teaching at the London AA school as the head of the Tropical Department in 1953, when Peter Smithson was a unit master there. Koenigsberger would also act as a climate design consultant to the Smithsons for their projects in Kuwait and Brazil. Another German influence comes from the writings of émigré architect Erwin Gutkind; both Gutkind and Koenigsberger had to flee from their home country due to the Nazi regime. In Britain Gutkind joined the MARS group, and gained fame with a series of essays on vernacular architecture for *Architectural Design* and a couple of books, in which he theorized the notion of environment, including *Community and Environment: A Discourse on Social Ecology* and *The Expanding Environment*, both published in 1953.[33]

French ethnology and geography and its relations to colonial survey have been quite extensively studied as an obvious source, especially in relation to the work of Candilis Josic Woods and the firm's indebtedness

**Van den Broek and Bakema,
Urban scheme for
Kennemerland region, 1959**

35   Jeanne Haffner, *The View from Above: The Science of Social Space*, (Cambridge, MA: MIT Press, 2013); a recent contribution to this field comes from Elisa Dainese, 'From the Charter of Athens to the "Habitat": CIAM 9 and the African Grids', *The Journal of Architecture* 3 (2019), 301-324.

36   Francis Strauven, *Aldo van Eyck: The Shape of Relativity* (Amsterdam: Architectura & Natura, 1998), 84-85.

37   Ibid., 243 and 352.

38   Alison and Peter Smithson, Dubrovnik Scroll, or Habitat 1956 manuscript, included in this publication on pages 22-25.

39   See Dirk van den Heuvel, 'Jaap Bakema en l'Exemple de Leeuwarden: Un Paysage Artificiel dans l'Infinité de l'Espace', in: Bruno Fayolle Lussac and Rémi Papillault (eds.), *Le Team X et le Logement Collectif à Grande Echelle en Europe: Un Retour Critique des Pratiques vers la Théorie* (Pessac: MSHA, 2008), 119-144.

40   For Aldo van Eyck's ideas on 'interiorization', see Chapter 11 in *Aldo van Eyck: Writings*, volume 'Collected Articles and Other Writings 1947-1998' (Amsterdam: SUN Publishers, 2008).

41   The term was originally coined by Liane Lefaivre and Alexander Tzonis, while regionalism as such was already discussed within the circles of modern architecture directly after the Second World War by, among others, Ludwig Hilberseimer and Sigfried Giedion.

to such formative figures as Michel Écochard, with whom Candilis and Woods had worked when in Morocco.[34] The impact of aerial photography – the view from above – is hard to underestimate here, a perfect tool for military control, it was soon appropriated by geographers for the survey of human settlements.[35] Gutkind too, used aerial photography to communicate the particularities of local traditions around the world.

Two other central figures that should be mentioned here – as examples of the transdisciplinary traffic going on – are Marcel Griaule and Martin Buber, who both profoundly impacted architectural thinking in the circles of the CIAM and Team 10, especially Aldo van Eyck. Griaule, a French anthropologist and a fighter pilot in the First and Second World Wars, would provide Van Eyck 's first introduction to the myths of the Dogon through a publication in Surrealist magazine *Minotaure*.[36] Buber, an Austrian-Jewish philosopher, incidentally wrote an introduction to Gutkind's book *Community and Environment*, and is best known for his philosophy of dialogue, which inspired both the older and the younger generations in the CIAM and Team 10. Buber's idea of a 'Gestalt gewordenes Zwischen' would inspire Rolf Gutmann and Theo Manz and incentivize Van Eyck to further his idea for the 'space between' in architecture.[37]

Landscape

One of the more intriguing aspects of the inclusion of the Valley Section in the Statement on Habitat is the implicit assumption regarding landscape as a precondition for urban design and architecture. In the many debates and documents, landscape as an explicit term is hardly present, however. Terms that were used to try and define habitat include territory, terrain, land, soil and environment. Other words are system, structure, cluster, association or pattern. Ecology is mentioned, just as ecological field and ecological setting. Alison and Peter Smithson briefly aim to theorize landscape in relation to habitat and ecology. It is a vignette-like diagram that is part of their 'Dubrovnik scroll', a document that summarized a series of their most pointed ideas under the header of 'Habitat 1956'. The particular diagram aims to explain the sliding scale between country and city. It speaks of 'country' as 'habitat in landscape', and 'city' as 'habitat is landscape'. The latter defines an anthropocene-like condition, in which the 'world' is impacted by planning and adjusted to make it fit for 'man'.[38]

Although the topic of landscape was neither recognized nor addressed explicitly at the Dubrovnik congress, it did appear in many of the presentations, not only in the Smithsons' contribution. The CIAM Porto

group showed a refined response to the hardships of rural life, while the grids of PAGON from Norway and PTAH from Finland demonstrated projects in dialogue with the landscape of their settings.

Also, among the Dutch contributions one can trace landscape concepts as part of the notion of habitat. Bakema's engagement with the Dutch landscape begins and ends with his reference to the vast, expansive polderscapes of Holland, and how the horizon and the trees are an orientational instrument for how to inhabit the landscape: under, above or between the trees. His monumental project for the urbanization of the Kennemerland region, presented in Otterlo at the last CIAM congress, forms the apotheosis. The various collages of the new modern landscape demonstrate an aesthetic sensibility that is firmly grounded in Dutch visual traditions, combining the drama of Dutch skies in Jacob van Ruisdael's landscape paintings with the elementary spatial concepts of *De Stijl*, most notably Piet Mondrian.[39]

Van Eyck's conceptualization of the interrelation between landscape, built environment and people is poetically captivated by his presentation of the design of the polder village of Nagele. On the first panel made for the Dubrovnik congress, a couple is depicted with their body contours formed by a montage of two photos of Dutch rural settlements. The images of church spires, birds, cows and waterscape were left unexplained, but seem to communicate Van Eyck's ideas on 'interiorization', a psychological process of identification by which the outside world is internalized by its inhabitants.[40]

It was the unknown architect and member of the Dutch CIAM group 'de 8 en Opbouw', Romke Romke de Vries, who engaged most explicitly with the characteristics of the Dutch landscape as ecology, at least in terms of its concrete material manifestations. Similar to the Valley Section, he presented a cross section of the Dutch delta landscape to demonstrate its nuanced differences due to the varying conditions of soil quality and water levels: from the dune landscapes along the coast, to the polders, dykes and canals, to the natural lakes, sandy areas and their forests, and the hills. The architecture fit for this landscape was one of a light touch, and lucid clarity. He used the work of Gerrit Rietveld, his son Jan, and his own to illustrate his point.

Habitat as 'Othering'

In the history of modern architecture, the polarity of centre and periphery remains a dominant concept. One response is the development of 'other' outsider positions, to both pluralize and criticize the established canon. Kenneth Frampton's proposition for a Critical Regionalism was one such attempt that was aimed against the rise of postmodernism in architecture, while focusing on overlooked modernist positions.[41] In more than one way, habitat belongs to such a practice of othering. The history of habitat as a specialist concept comes with all sorts of colonial overtones of so-called discovery and survey, which in fact are often the beginnings of subjugation, appropriation and exploitation. What happens when such concepts are brought to the centre? Or as Peter Smithson has suggested: 'From the rain-forest into the streets.'[42]

In architecture, the term habitat was initially associated with the vernacular, the rural, the unlearned, the primitive and assumedly unconscious culture. Lina Bo Bardi's magazine *Habitat* might be considered a case in point, but also Aldo van Eyck's fascination for the Dogon culture and people. To use habitat to reconceptualize Western, Eurocentric urban design and the field of housing might thus be considered an act of provocation. Because conventionally, Architecture with a capital A is considered a part of the domains of culture, self-consciousness and enlightenment. Although it was surely intended to expand and transform the discipline, despite being motivated as a gesture of appreciation and acknowledgement, or even as a project of emancipation, can habitat as an architectural term move beyond those aspects of exoticization?

Dutch Regionalism?

In the history of Team 10, the contributions from Portugal, Scandinavia and Central and Eastern Europe have indeed often been framed as peripheral.[43] Is some form of reversal possible here? What would happen if we were to use Frampton's idea of 'regionalization' to reposition Portuguese and Scandinavian architecture, but also English architecture, to speculate on the Dutch contributions to Team 10 and the Dubrovnik congress?

This question formed the incentive for a closer look at the holdings in the National Collection and to search for critical continuities of the Team 10 discourse in terms of habitat and ecology thinking. The selected projects and designers originate from the milieu of the Faculty of Architecture of Delft University of Technology, and its circle of modern architecture professors: Johannes van den Broek and Cornelis van Eesteren, the chairman of the CIAM (1930-1947), who were appointed in the late 1940s, and Jaap Bakema and Aldo van Eyck in the mid-1960s. Pjotr Gonggrijp is presented as an unknown yet key figure, who was an assistant to both Van Eesteren and Van Eyck. He made

his fame with his thesis project for the analysis and redesigning of the Dutch delta. Joost Váhl was perhaps one of the first activist-ecologists in urban planning who campaigned in favour of biodiversity. As a young Delft graduate he became involved in redeveloping the southern expansion scheme for Delft, Tanthof, which was designed by the Van den Broek and Bakema office. To develop an alternative scheme that respected the existing polder landscape, Váhl joined the Tanthof working group, which also included Frans Hooykaas and Peter Lüthi of Van den Broek and Bakema, and Anneloes van den Berg and Hiwe Groenewolt. Urban designer Frits Palmboom is of a younger generation, as a student he was influenced by Gonggrijp's lectures and landscape analyses, while he himself also acknowledges the impact of Team 10 thinking – Bakema and Van Eyck, but particularly the Smithsons.[44] In addition, two regional studies from the late 1980s are included, which display a specific environmental awareness: one project by Willem Jan Neutelings, the so-called Patchwork Metropolis, and a scenario for 2050 by Peter Terreehorst for the coast of the Dutch province of Zeeland.[45]

What conclusions might be drawn from the selections? The following propositions could be regarded as central to habitat as ecology thinking.

Habitat as Matter

First of all, habitat not only involves material aspects of the environment, it is literally matter, the land, the mud and the sand, the dikes and the canals, but also the vegetation, the reed, the grass and trees. After all, the Dutch peatlands are nothing but vegetational sedimentation. This is also the proposition of Romke de Vries: to look at habitat from the view of different landscape typologies and soil and water conditions.

Gonggrijp's painstaking drawings document the transformative impact of human occupation on landscape formation. His drawings suggest that the spatial configurations of the patterns of inhabitation cannot be uncoupled from the material qualities of the land. Such awareness of ecological coherence also comes to the fore in Palmboom's interpretation of the landscape around Alphen aan de Rijn. Equally astute is his observation of the occurrence of incoherence and disruption as in the case of the Rotterdam cityscape. Such profoundly material understanding of the environment and habitat can also be perceived in the straightforward proposals of Joost Váhl, which are written like recipes to also locally achieve a biodiverse environment that can be enjoyed by touching, smelling and even eating, by growing food and herbs in public parks and greens.

Aldo van Eyck, playground Zaanhof, Amsterdam, 1948

RAAAF and Barbara Visser, *The End of Sitting,* Amsterdam, 2014

Jaap Bakema, diagram of 'transitional elements', 1964

42   Mark Crinson, 'From the Rainforest to the Streets', in: Tom Avermaete, Serhat Karakayali and Marion von Osten (eds.), *Colonial Modern: Aesthetics of the Past, Rebellions for the Future* (London: Black Dog Publishing, 2010), 99-111.

43   Much of the new research positions itself critically towards this historiographical argument, for instance the conference and publication *Team 10 East* organized by Łukasz Stanek and Aleksandra Kedziorek in 2013-2014, in Warsaw, and the Portuguese-Spanish research network Team Ten Farwest, which organized conferences in Guimaraes, Barcelona and Porto between 2017 and 2020 (teamtenfarwest.com). To revisit the congress of Dubrovnik 1956 was initiated by, among others, Ivan Rupnik and Renate Margaretic Urlic for their project 'Living CIAM X Dubrovnik 1956-2016', which included a three-day seminar and an exhibition at the Museum of Modern Art in Dubrovnik.

44   For the exhibition project, various conversations took place between the author and these actors. Two public seminars with interviews were organized in early 2019 at Het Nieuwe Instituut, Rotterdam.

45   Terreehorst is the only person not from Delft University of Technology, but from Wageningen University. The larger project in which Terreehorst participated was initiated by planner Dirk Frieling, who was a professor in Delft.

46   See Erik Rietveld and Janno Martens' text in this publication, page128-135.

47   For an overview, see: Arnulf Lüchinger, *Structuralism in Architecture and Urban Planning* (Stuttgart: Karl Krämer Verlag, 1981).

48   In conversation with the author.

Crucially, it also means that habitat as landscape is not to be reduced to an aesthetic experience, it is also a corporeal experience. At least, this is how these designers themselves talk about it: how one moves through the various landscape conditions, to be close to the water, to feel protected or exposed, how weather affects the human body, and also how the view of the open horizon – the typical Dutch expanse of water bodies under clouded skies – is a moment of becoming aware of bodily immersion, an encounter with an almost cosmological endlessness.

Subcultures and Lifestyles

In close connection with such material understanding of habitat one might observe a striking interest in the treatment of surfaces and textures, and how in the words of Erik Rietveld of the RAAAF office these provide so-called affordances that enable specific patterns of use and appropriation.[46] At the heart of habitat as ecological thinking is the recognition of this interrelationship between 'men and things' as first proposed and theorized by Jaap Bakema in 1951. It is also a performative understanding of habitat, which becomes immediately clear from Aldo van Eyck's designs for urban playgrounds. Such reciprocity between spatial-material configuration and performance is also found in the installations of RAAAF, such as the End of Sitting and Breaking Habits. There seems to be a common understanding that from this dynamic interaction between inhabitants and their habitat, specific subcultures and lifestyles emerge, and how they might amalgamate into new fluid, hybrid identities. Perhaps superfluous to point out, but here, we touch on one the key concepts behind Structuralism in architecture as it was developed in Team 10 discussions, in dialogue or opposition.[47]

Multiple Systems

One of the more complicated issues to understand is how habitat is not just one ecological system, but how it emerges from and combines multiple systems. Gonggrijp is fully engaged in this, especially so in the case of his peculiar transhistorical maps that combine different periods and time frames into one image. Historical Dutch towns of the seventeenth century are, for instance, combined with the modern infrastructure of the twentieth century while leaving out the intermediate developments.

We see this also in the contributions of Palmboom and Neutelings, albeit in almost opposite ways. This recognition of multiple systems working

together (or not) is not only about difference and diversity, nor is it about tracing the paradoxes that make up the modern cityscape, it also concerns the understanding of the impact of scale and the continuation of hierarchies (the *longue durée* of climate and geology versus the event of human technology, for instance), in space and in time.

'Playing with Modernity'

A final observation concerns how habitat is also a thoroughly modern term. Behind the modest and careful approaches there is a not so modest ambition to capture the human habitat in its full extent – as the 'whole problem of environment'. The drawings of Gonggrijp, which meticulously record human patterns, are simultaneously an investigation into the accommodation of new large-scale port facilities for Rotterdam, and equally expansive regional housing clusters. Drawings not only identify the characteristics of the Dutch delta landscape, they also propose its profound transformation. One of the maps has the whole of the North Sea basin as its subject, an aspirational redesign of the area between the urban configurations of London, Paris and Hamburg, with the Dutch Randstad at its centre. Other drawings show studies of migration patterns on the European continent, of people and of birds. Numbers and how to organize groups of numbers to make them live together, is at the core of Gonggrijp's thinking.

In the future scenario for the province of Zeeland, we see a much more practical but still challenging approach. The maps are like examples of a geography lesson from school, blue is for water and the sea, yellow for the blond sand dunes, and dark green for the forests. And yet, these maps present the tremendously transformative capacity of the notion of habitat. In a mere three steps Terreehorst recreates the coast of Zeeland, a full integration of the marine landscape, the dunes and the flood defence system, the new suburban areas, leisure facilities and agri-food industry, fit for the twenty-first century.

To accommodate change is part and parcel of the idea of habitat for Palmboom. He speaks of 'playing with modernity', almost as if it is an innocent game, an unusually light-hearted statement for such a thoroughly serious designer.[48] The notion of 'playing' betrays a ludic tradition, that might be called Dutch. It certainly resists an essentialist understanding of habitat, and bypasses ideological dogma, while it acknowledges the dynamic reciprocity that is at stake between habitat and inhabitants. Such a dynamic irreversibly instigates transformation, a generative process from which wholly new environments will be created.

Aerial view of Dubrovnik

HABITAT 1956

Dubrovnik Scroll by
Alison and Peter Smithson

The so-called Dubrovnik Scroll is a document compiled by Alison and Peter Smithson to summarize their ideas on the notion of habitat. It was prepared especially for the CIAM conference in Dubrovnik and brings together various statements by the Smithsons from the period 1952 to 1956. In many ways it can be considered their proposition for a Charter of Habitat. The version kept in the archives of Het Nieuwe Instituut is apparently one that was used for various publication purposes, witness the many editorial annotations on the document.

The Smithsons identified four key terms to explain their understanding of the notion of habitat: identity, association, cluster and mobility. These are printed in bold lettering at the bottom of the document and then summed up with the phrase 'the whole problem of environment'. The Smithsons theorized these terms in their extensive writings of the 1950s, for instance in relation to their well-known manifesto-like housing project Golden Lane, which they had presented at the CIAM conference in 1953. The two terms of identity and human association are related to the sociocultural issues pertaining to the habitat question. They build up into and accommodate patterns of inhabitations, the spatial and architectural configurations that can sustain communities over time. Even when historical precedent is part of the Smithsons' interest, the forms of modern life are not to simply repeat the old ones. Patterns of associations are to be translated into 'new types', of 'ways of coming together'. In search of a new vocabulary, the term 'cluster' is then introduced as a general, open term, unburdened by 'historical overtones'.

The fourth term of 'mobility' complicates 'the whole problem of environment'. Mobility stands for the condition of modernity and the new realities of consistent change and disruption. To the Smithsons, mobility revolved around a new kind of freedom, not only in terms of movement but also in terms of social progress, an advancement to an egalitarian, welfare state society free of the limits imposed by a class society. Yet, the complexities that derive from the uncoupling of territory, traditional notions of belonging and social interaction through mobility are not something the Smithsons seem to have found problematic. They stated, for instance, that 'association does not necessarily mean contact', when they referred to the development of the new mass media. At this stage in their career they embraced the resulting new dynamic, being fascinated by 'mobility as sensation'.

Besides environment, communications and complexity, another striking term used is 'ecology'. A diagram explains the reciprocities between existing ecologies and change, and the ones between habitat and landscape. In 1956, the Smithsons concluded that one precondition for such reciprocity is the definition and provision of a 'basic structure' that allows 'for maximum freedom for growth and change'.

Alison and Peter Smithson

Leonardo Zuccaro Marchi

BETWEEN *HABITER* AND HABITAT

CIAM and the Sigtuna Meeting of 1952

CIAM, 'Réunion du Conseil et des Délégués de Groupes à Sigtuna', June 1952

1   Hadas A. Steiner, 'After Habitat, Environment', *New Geographies 06: Grounding Metabolism* (2014), 89.
2   Reyner Banham, *The Architecture of the Well-tempered Environment* (Chicago: University of Chicago Press, 1969), 143.
3   Fred Forbat, 1952, ArkDes Stockholm, Am 1970-18.
4   There were 59 attendants, according to *Le Documents de Sigtuna*, 65 according to a letter from Josep Lluis Sert to Sigfried Giedion, 12 June 1952, Fondation Le Corbusier, Paris, D219/251 -01-02-03; and according to a letter from Josep Lluis Sert to Fred Forbat, 17 June 1952, ArkDes Archive, Stockholm, AM 1970-18.
5   See D. Grahame Shane, 'The Street in the Twentieth Century: Three Conferences: London (1910), Athens (1933), Hoddesdon (1951)', *The Cornell Journal of Architecture* 2 (1983), 41.

6   Jaqueline Tyrwhitt, in: CIAM, *Les Documents de Sigtuna*, 1952, ArkDes Stockholm, Am 1970-18.
7   Christian Norberg-Schulz, 'On the Creation of Junior Groups', Sigtuna, 26 June 1952, Fondation Le Corbusier, D2-19-78-001 / 42-JT-10-70, gta/ETH. CIAM, Le Documents de Sigtuna.
8   CIAM, letter from the CIAM Extraordinary Council Meeting, Paris, 14 May 1952, GSD Harvard, CIAM Collection C11.
9   Giedion, 28 June 1952, in: CIAM, *Le Documents de Sigtuna*, op. cit. (note 6).
10   CIAM, *Les Documents de Sigtuna*, 5 and 10.
11   André Wogenscky, letter to Josep Lluis Sert, Paris, 9 April 1953, Bakema Archive (g21, BAKE0153), Het Nieuwe Instituut, Rotterdam.

The rethinking of architecture through the lens of habitat gained momentum in the post-war urban discourse of the Congrès Internationaux d'Architecture Moderne (CIAM, 1928-1959) and it has subsequently revolutionized architecture and urban design theory. The watershed notion of habitat implied an alternative urban vocabulary to former accepted categories. In particular, by introducing ecological thinking in architectural discussions, it challenged and superseded the analytical pre-war dictates of the concept of the Functional City that the CIAM had promulgated through its Athens Charter of 1933. It caused the cultural shift within design and theory from *habiter* to habitat, 'from 'oikos' – house to 'oecology' – ecology'.[1] As such, it fostered the passage from a sectorial-functionalist focus on the singular, isolated urban functions to an interest in the interdependent relationships between domestic space and its environment, from a universalist approach to a focus on regional variations, local cultural identities, regional landscape and urban differences, also in the non-Western contexts peripheral to the debates in Europe and North America.

This pivotal and revolutionizing turn towards habitat was not first tackled at one of the official CIAM conferences, the forum of 'the official Establishment of architecture' as British historian Reyner Banham caustically put it.[2] The epistemological shift rather commenced during a minor preparatory meeting of the CIAM held at the Humanistika School in Sigtuna, Sweden, from 25 June to 30 June 1952. Though conceived as an interim meeting of the CIAM council and delegates, Sigtuna turned into a salient 'so alive small Congress'.[3] It counted at least 59 participants.[4] It fostered a transitory debate between the CIAM 8 congress of 1951 in Hoddesdon, and CIAM 9, planned for 1953 in Aix-en-Provence, and their organicist themes of respectively the 'Heart of the City' and the 'Charter of Habitat'. Thus, not only did Sigtuna represent an 'in-between' moment in the official CIAM history, it also brought to the fore the conceptualization of habitat as a relational category in terms of architecture and planning theory. The philosophy of Martin Buber, which had gained quite some popularity in those years, also among architects, was highly influential here, as we will see.

Tellingly, the debates at the five-day Sigtuna meeting started to reveal radical disagreements among CIAM members, between different interpretations of *habiter* and habitat, as well as between the CIAM manifestos, particularly the Athens Charter and the planned Charter of Habitat. The ensuing disputes continued in the following years until the final collapse of the CIAM in 1959, which for some also marked the collapse of modern architecture itself.[5] This rift also coincided with a new and urgently demanded balance of roles between young and old 'creators' among CIAM members.[6] Facing both the problematic formation of junior groups and the lack of clear statements by the original founders, young Norwegian architect Christian Norberg-Schulz polemically questioned in Sigtuna: 'Why do we join CIAM?'[7]

Between *Habiter* and Habitat

Regarding the acceptance of the term habitat, the preference between habitat and *habiter* was controversially linked to the uses, meanings and fields of interpretation in each language and culture. French was still the main language of discussion among CIAM participants, and the language of the report of the proceedings, *Les documents de Sigtuna.* However, the English term 'dwelling', the French *logis* or *habitation*, the Italian *abitare,* etcetera, were not considered to be interchangeable. In fact, during the meeting held in Paris the preceding month, on 14 May 1952, the CIAM Council had already admitted that 'the word "Habitat" is difficult to translate into English'.[8] In Sigtuna, Ernesto Nathan Rogers proposed to employ the Italian *Carta dell'Abitare*, while other members, such as the former CIAM chair Cornelis van Eesteren, considered that a certain conjunction between the English and French meaning of the word habitat was possible, particularly regarding their biological connotation and, beyond this, evoking 'the spirit of the place where it is located'.[9] Still, the wish to investigate the meanings of habitat was continuously hindered by the different attitudes, preconceptions and references embedded in each cultural background. The significance and multiple nuances of the term were grounded in the cultural setting of each international CIAM member participating in Sigtuna. Their culturally divergent ways of organizing and conceiving of the built environment enhanced ambiguity and misunderstanding.

Significantly, the choice of the right term was felt to be an important and crucial obligation with radical consequences beyond the culturally exclusive and elitist circle of the CIAM. According to Ioannis Despotopoulos, the prominent and international role of the CIAM necessitated the adoption of clear ideas and terminologies, since these would influence entire populations and 'the conception which men will have about the city',[10] thus imbuing the debate with a sense of social responsibility.

Nevertheless, despite – or because of – this social-linguistic concern, in Sigtuna the discussion could not avoid a deep 'language dispute about the word Habitat', as André Wogenscky later admitted to Josep Lluis Sert in 1953 in a letter imbued with irritation.[11] The struggle to distinguish between habitat

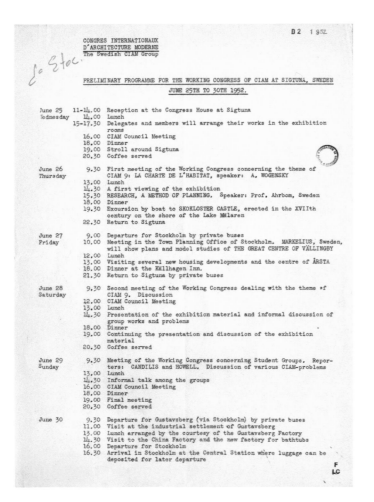

Preliminary programme for the working Congress of CIAM at Sigtuna, early 1952

Programme of the meeting, in *Les Documents de Sigtuna*, June 1952

12   CIAM, *Les Documents de Sigtuna*, op. cit. (note 6), 3.

13   André Wogenscky, letter to Fred Forbat, 22 February 1952, Arkdes Stockholm, Forbat Archive Am 1970-18.

14   Francis Strauven, *Aldo van Eyck: The Shape of Relativity* (Amsterdam: Architectura & Natura, 1998), 241.

15   Walter Gropius, letter to Fred Forbat, 20 March 1952, ArkDes Stockholm, Am 1970-18.

16   See Eric Mumford, *The CIAM Discourse on Urbanism, 1928-1960* (Cambridge, MA: MIT Press, 2000), 329, note 88.

17   See Tom Avermaete, *Acculturating the Modern: Candilis-Josic-Woods and the Epistemological Shift in Post-War Architecture and Urbanism* (PhD Thesis, Leuven University, 2004), 63-64.

18   André Wogenscky, Reunion Inaugurale Du Congres De Travail, Mercredi Le 25 Juin, 18.00, in: CIAM, *Le Documents de Sigtuna*, op. cit. (note 6).

and *habitation* had its own supporters and opponents. The two contrasting sides almost corresponded with the generational divide between the old-CIAM founders and the young members, who were eager to take up a new position within the congress. As portrayed by Vilhelm Lauritzen there were two protagonists of this severe and harsh opposition: the abovementioned Wogenscky and Georges Candilis, one of the exponents of the future Team 10 group.[12] Wogenscky acted as the official representative of Le Corbusier in Sigtuna and he would plea for *habitation* as the central concept.[13] Tellingly, Candilis too had worked for Le Corbusier, who himself had in fact urged for a discussion on habitat before, in 1949 during the seventh CIAM conference held in Bergamo, Italy.

Still, for Wogenscky *habitation* was methodologically conceived as the proper term, encompassing both a definition broader than mere dwelling and a context more precise than the vague notion of habitat. In opposition to this, the young members were critical of the fact that for Le Corbusier the term *habitation* merely constituted an ample development of the pre-war *habiter*, as 'the pure undiluted "dwelling" of the Athens Charter'.[14] In contrast, they recognized the complexity of the ecological content of habitat as a sociobiological theoretical framework that focused on the sociospatial relationships of human settlements.

From this ecological perspective, habitat had to be considered within a broader interdisciplinary, cultural milieu, avoiding the 'sort of intellectual CIAM incest' as described by Walter Gropius.[15] As at previous CIAM meetings, in Sigtuna Gropius highlighted the urgency for a much more multidisciplinary approach with sociologists, psychologists and biologists also taking part in the discussion on habitat. Yet, even when in Sweden this interdisciplinary attendance was missing, the CIAM's cultural 'incest' did not preclude the rich sociological and philosophical influences and references on both sides of the dispute.

Wogenscky: *Habiter* as Everyday Life

On Thursday 26 June, during the first meeting of the Congres de Travail, chaired by Lauritzen, André Wogenscky immediately focused the attention on the need to consider *habitation* rather than habitat as the main topic. To him, the term habitat had too vast a meaning, both in English and in French, encompassing several fields of knowledge such as sociology, human geography and political economy. Slightly in contradiction with the aforementioned denouncement of Gropius against a monodisciplinary approach, the French architect deemed that the aim of the CIAM was

to discuss only ideas and terms with operative and useful roles for the design work of architects, though he conceded that their interdisciplinary complexity was to be taken into account as well. Hence, Wogenscky suggested that *habitation* seemed to perfectly mirror this balance, at least in the French language. He underlined that even though *habitation* primarily means 'house' or 'dwelling', in French its meaning also encompasses the 'daily place where the family lives' (*lieu quotidien où vit la famille*). As such, the term *habitation* was considered to carry both the individual and collective spheres of dwelling and all its extensions: commercial, hygienic, educational, social and administrative. On the one hand, the French *habitation* was exhibited with broader connotations than in other languages, causing contrast and confusion. On the other, Wogenscky specifically redirected the issue of habitat-*habiter* towards the concrete presence of the 'everyday life' that betrayed a familiarity with the contemporary, social critique of Henri Lefebvre.[16]

It implied an important epistemological shift from the abstract understanding of sociological, geographic and economic realities towards their concrete contingencies.[17] *Habiter* was thus embedded within everyday practices not restricted to the interior space of the private sphere of dwelling, but extending to its surroundings, to social life. This broader – French-grounded – idea of *habiter* was even more heightened by Wogenscky in Sigtuna, when he specifically interpreted the French *habitation* as:

> ...an indivisible whole... – *a tout indivisible* – ...a structure, a form, a 'Gestalt'...that means something unique, a whole that ceases to exist when one of its parts is suppressed. In all reality the housing elements are intimately related.[18]

Between its French use and its reference to the German *Gestalt* philosophy, the individual and collective spheres of habitation had be considered as a complete form, as a totality, which couldn't match with any functionalist separation of the city elements as commanded by the pre-war ideology of the CIAM. Paradoxically, these interpretations were later expanded, even more forcefully, by the same young members who vehemently criticized Wogenscky at the Sigtuna conference.

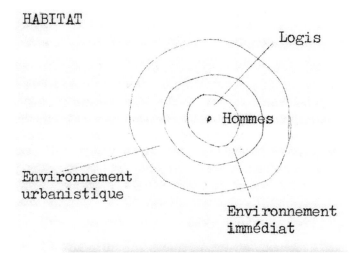

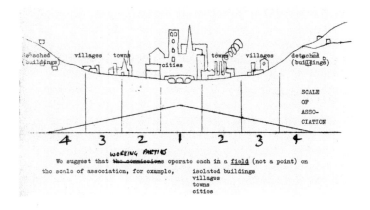

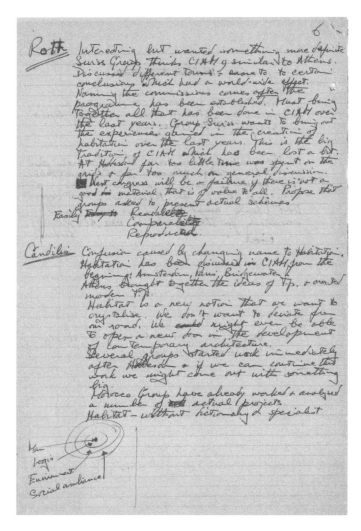

Georges Candilis, 'Habitat', June 1952

Team 10, 'Scale of Association', 1954

Georges Candilis's 'Habitat' in Tyrwhitt's notes, June 1952

19   Georges Candilis, 'Habitat', *Encyclopaedia Universalis* (Paris, 1969), 193. Quotd in Tom Avermaete, *Another Modern: The Post-War Architecture and Urbanism of Candilis-Josic-Woods* (Rotterdam: NAi Publishers, 2005), 143.

20   CIAM, *Les Documents de Sigtuna*, op. cit. (note 6).

21   Georges Candilis and Jaqueline Tyrwhitt, 'Habitat without Dictionary', June 1952, gta/ETH Zurich, 42-JT-10/142.

22   'Discussion on organizational matters Doorn, 29 January 1954, (evening)', in: Allison Smithson (ed.), *The Emergence of Team 10 out of CIAM* (London: AAGS Theory and History Papers 1.82, Architectural Association, 1982), see also Mumford, *The CIAM Discourse on Urbanism*, op. cit. (note 16), 224; and Annie Pedret, *Team 10: An Archival History*, (Abingdon: Routledge, 2013), 81-82.

23   In CIAM, *Les Documents de Sigtuna*, op. cit. (note 6).

24   Martin Buber, *Ich un Du* (Leipzig: Insel-Verlag, 1923). Translated by Walter Kaufmann as *I and Thou: A New Translation* (New York: Charles Scribner's Sons, 1970).

25   Martin Buber, *Das Problem des Menschen* (1948), cited in: Joop Hardy and Herman Hertzberger, 'Drempel en ontmoeting: de gestalte van het tussen', *Forum* 8 (1959), 249.

26   Regarding Buber's influence on modern architects see: Ellen Shoshkes, 'East-West: Interactions between the United States and Japan and Their Effect on Utopian Realism', *Journal of Planning History* 3 (2004), 215-240.

27   Strauven, *Aldo van Eyck*, op. cit. (note 14), 243.

28   Jaap Bakema, 'Relationship Between Men and Things', in: Jaqueline Tyrwhitt, Josep Lluis Sert, Ernesto Nathan Rogers (eds.), *The Heart of the City: Towards the Humanisation of Urban Life* (London: L. Humphries, 1952), 67.

29   Leonardo Zuccaro Marchi, *The Heart of the City: Legacy and Complexity of a Modern Design Idea* (London: Routledge, 2018), 149-184; Dirk van den Heuvel (ed.), *Jaap Bakema and the Open Society* (Amsterdam: Archis, 2018).

30   Interestingly, Gutmann and Manz were present at CIAM 8 in Hoddesdon, but did not personally attend the Sigtuna meeting.

Candilis: The Ecological Habitat

Georges Candilis burst into the discussion stressing explicitly the confusion and inappropriateness of the use of *habitation* rather than habitat, which to him jeopardized the main purpose of the meeting. He argued that *habitation* had already been deeply discussed in many CIAM meetings before, and the Charter of Habitat should propose a new urban concept. Furthermore, according to Candilis only the notion of habitat was conceptually and semantically able to embrace both the specific private dwelling practice and its cultural, climatic and territorial surroundings, in a perpetual intermediation between different types of human needs and their context. Habitat had to be adopted 'in the broadest ecological sense of the term, that is, the overall environment in which humanity dwells.[19]

In Sigtuna – which incidentally was also the cultural milieu of Carl Linnaeus who was probably the first to introduce the term habitat in his *Systema Naturae* (1735) – Candilis synthesized the broader ecological meaning of habitat by drawing a scheme on the blackboard accompanied by French terms. This scheme consisted of three concentric circles with 'human beings' (*Hommes*) at the centre, 'Dwelling' (*Logis*) around it, followed by the 'immediate environment' (*environnement immediate*) and finally, the 'urban environment' (*environnement urbanistique*) encompassed all the circles.[20] Even though he gave no further explanations, his diagram aimed to shift the interest from the topic of dwelling as an isolated function to a more relational centrality on the thresholds between the human being and its living environments.

The same scheme was also included in the notes written in English by Jaqueline Tyrwhitt; *Logis* remained in French, *environnement immédiat* was simply translated as 'environment', while *environnement urbanistique* was transmuted to 'social ambience', shifting the notion of the urban towards a more specific social concept.[21] As already emphasized, the different languages engendered variations, nuances and slippery misunderstandings that intensified the ambiguity and complexity of the discourse on habitat. Besides these different interpretations, translations and variations, Candilis's scheme can doubtlessly be considered as the first schematic representation of habitat by a future Team 10 member. In particular, his concentric scheme anticipated the 'Scale of Association' proposed by Team 10 in 1954 in the Doorn Manifesto, which would definitively supersede the sectorial-functional diktats of the Athens Charter. While Candilis's circular scheme raised a broader ecological sense of habitat involving the interdependency between private dwelling and external urban spheres, in the Doorn Manifesto, the new scale levels – from the isolated buildings, villages and towns to the metropolis – brought to the fore the sociospatial complex structures of the built environment as a counterforce to its sectorial-analytical division, as previously enshrined in the Athens Charter and the idea of the Functional City. All in all, the 'confused and troublesome' Sigtuna meeting – as recalled by Aldo Van Eyck in Doorn in 1954 – disclosed and anticipated the main character and theoretical assumptions of the later Team 10, even becoming a manifesto of the 'prehistory of Team 10'.[22]

Habitat as In-Between

In Sigtuna, the ecological emphasis on habitat as a counterforce to any functionalist division and compartmentalisation of the built environment opened the debate to other references and theories that would be formative to the thinking of Team 10. In particular, the young architects from Basel, Rolf Gutmann and Theo Manz, should be mentioned here. They submitted the paper 'La Charte de l'Habitat: Ueberlegungen über das Wesen des Themas', (The Habitat Charter: Reflections on the Nature of the Topic) in which they adopted and elaborated Martin Buber's theory of the 'in-between'.[23] The Austrian Jewish philosopher and author of *Ich und Du* (*I and Thou*, 1923) was the founder of a theory grounded on the notions of relationship and dialogue as the counterforce to isolation and monologue.[24] In this existentialist philosophy based on the human encounter, the 'sphere of the in-between' was considered the primary category of human reality and a fundamental condition of human beings with their fellow human beings.[25]

The influences and resonances of the 'in-between' had already been spreading in modern architecture circles.[26] Dutch architect Aldo van Eyck, who graduated from the ETH Zurich, had been familiar with the notion of the 'in-between' since his childhood, in particular through poetry.[27] One year before Sigtuna, at CIAM 8 in Hoddesdon, Jaap Bakema had proposed the idea of the sociospatial encounter by interpreting the conference theme of the 'Heart of the City' as one of a total relationship, in Bakema's words as the 'wonder of relationship between man and things'. Describing the moment of 'core', he evoked a sense of collective awareness 'of the fullness of life by means of cooperative action', which evolves within a 'dynamic continuity'.[28] Somehow, the symbolical abstract and organic interpretation of the 'Heart of the City' theme heralded a broader ecological idea of habitat as a relational paradigm for the human settlement, as later developed within Team 10.[29]

Gutmann and Manz reiterated this idea of the dynamic relationship of the Heart of the City.[30]

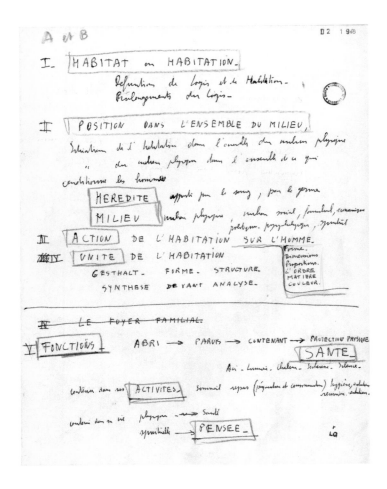

Front and back of a postcard to Giedion, with a reassuring message from Stockholm: 'Dear Professor, CIAM develops fine, do not bother about it. Cordially', June 1952

Notes of Le Corbusier and André Wogenscky, 1952

31 Martin Buber, 'Urdistanz und Bezichung', in: Rolf Gutmann, and Theo Manz, 'La Charte de l'Habitat: Ueberlegungen *über* das Wesen des Themas', in: CIAM, *Les Documents de Sigtuna*, op. cit. (note 6); and *Forum 7* (1959), 215.

32 gta/ETH Zurich, CIAM42-WM-X-7.

33 Annie Pedret, 'Representing History or Describing Historical Reality? The Universal and the Individual in the 1950s', in: Pekka Korvennaa and Esa Laaksonen (eds.), *Universal Versus Individual: The Architecture of the 1960s* (Helsinki/Jyväskylä: Alvar Aalto Academy/Alvar Aalto Museum/University of Art and Design, 2002), 82-85.

34 Tom Avermaete and Maristella Casciato, *Casablanca Chandigarh: A Report on Modernization* (Montreal/Zurich: Canadian Center for Architecture/Park Books, 2014).

35 Mumford, *The CIAM Discourse on Urbanism,* op. cit. (note 16), 221.

36 Le Corbusier, 9 May 1955, in: Smithson, *The Emergence of Team 10 out of CIAM*, op. cit. (note 22), 47.

37 Henri Lefebvre, *The Urban Revolution* (Minneapolis/London: University of Minnesota Press, 2003), 81. Originally published in French: Henri Lefebvre, *La revolution urbaine* (Paris: Gallimard, 1970).

38 Ibid. For a discussion on the French definition of *habiter*-habitat see Thierry Paquot, 'Habitat, habitation, habiter, Ce que parler veut dire...' Caisse nationale d'allocations familiales (CNAF), *Informations sociales* 123/3 (2005), 48-54.

Acknowledgements
This text is the result of my postdoc research at KTH Stockholm in 2014-2015. An extended version of this text, entitled 'Sigtuna In-between: The First Architectural Dispute on Habitat', was awarded with an honourable mention in the Bruno Zevi Prize competition in 2016. I am warmly grateful for the advice and support of Helena Mattsson at KTH University, Stockholm and for the archive help of Erik Sigge (KTH) and Andreas Kalpakci (ETH Zurich).

They embraced the design of the in-between, called *Zwischen* by Buber, as an essential feature of the habitat paradigm: 'Art is neither the impression of natural objectivity, nor the expression of soulful subjectivity; it is work and witness to the relation between the *substantia humana* and the *substantia rerum*, the in-between that has taken place.'[31]

Gutmann and Manz proposed a vision of the dwelling as a synergistic part of the human settlement, studying the various relationships within the design of the in-between. In their view, the CIAM should not have conceived the dwelling as an isolated function, but as a constituent and integrating element of the rest of the human settlement as a whole – interestingly, thus sharing many similarities with Wogenscky's *Gestalt* definition of *habiter*. Hence, the compartmentalized methods of 'analysis' and planning – adopted for instance with CIAM's grid – should be substituted by more inclusive and 'synthetisizing' points of view that understand the complexity of the various relationships of the human settlement as 'a whole, a living whole'.[32] The organic habitat as 'in-between' prefigures Team 10's research on 'the shape of the in-between' in the 1950s and 1960s. It critically challenged the sectorial, analytical division of the pre-war Functional City concept and its homogenizing, universalist approach.[33] Gutmann and Manz's proposition initiated a broader approach in architecture and urban design thinking, allowing for a more inclusive approach to the planning of the territory, one that considered the built environment as a coherent, complex ecological-anthropological system, with a new attention to the local cultural identities and regional landscapes.[34]

Convergences and Continuing Disputes

In response to the dispute between *habiter* and habitat, Lauritzen calmed the tension in the session by stressing that Wogenscky's *habitation* seemed very similar to Candilis's habitat. Indeed, Wogenscky's plea for everyday life seemed consistent with Candilis's ecological notion of human association. They both introduced a new social and ecological focus in the architectural and urban design debate, grounding *habiter*-habitat within a specific linguistic and cultural use, and allowing for contamination by other disciplines. Moreover, both positions were aimed at developing and further improving the discourse on dwelling within its post-war humanist conception, rather than referring to the pre-war functionalist discourse. Even if the opposition in Sigtuna was much less evident, as suggested by the CIAM participants themselves, the 'wide-ranging and unfocused' language dispute was destined to continue.[35] Three years later,

in 1955, Le Corbusier famously tried to 'suppress all misunderstanding' between 'Habitat, *Habiter, habitation* (in French) and Habitat, living, dwelling or home (in English)', offering a final, resolute 'formula' in both languages: '*L'Habitat represente les condition de vie dans le milieu total.*' (The Habitat represents the condition of life (the accommodation, the function) in the total environment.)[36] However, his attempt was not enough to patch up both the deep conceptual and generational rift within the CIAM and the emergent Team 10, a divide that manifested in Sigtuna for the first time.

Interestingly, as late as 1970 in his *La révolution urbaine*, Henri Lefebvre would return to the semiotic gulf between *habiter* and habitat and stress its relevance and utility: 'Although the distinction between "habiting" and "habitat" is already subject to considerable controversy, I still insist that it is useful.'[37] Lefebvre vehemently criticized habitat as a 'caricatural pseudo-concept', a reductive functionalist urban thought that 'was imposed from above as the application of a homogeneous global and quantitative space'. Contrarily, he praised habiting as an ancestral 'functional, multifunctional and transfunctional' activity, 'as a source of foundation'.[38] Hence, Lefebvre seemed to subvert and invert the CIAM critiques on *habiter*-habitat, heightening even more the slippery ambiguity of the language dispute between Wogenscky and Candilis. More importantly, this later interdisciplinary reiteration of the debate highlights the pioneering role of the Sigtuna meeting in the search for a new theoretical vocabulary to understand the post-war urban condition and to operate in it. The socially responsible and harshly disputed development of a new urban ecological lexicon – captured by the new term of habitat – appears to be the most important legacy of Sigtuna, and remains an important point of reference for the understanding of our contemporary urban condition as well.

SOCIAL SPACES

Presentations at CIAM 10 – Micro-scale

Among the designs presented at the Dubrovnik conference there is a series that intensely engages with the small scale and the local as the unique site to create specific identities from which a feeling of belonging and community could grow. The proposed spatial configurations were often derived from the study of historical and regional precedents with a special interest for intermediate spaces that allow for the negotiation between the private and public realm, while accommodating social encounter. In line with Patrick Geddes's Valley Section, proposals involved a broad range of contexts, from the rural and the suburban to the metropolitan. Each proposal aimed to come up with a solution tailored to the situation and the contemporary problems of city planning and housing.

The presentations by the British MARS (Modern Architecture Research) group include a set of modest interventions for new housing schemes in rural regions. Taking inspiration from picturesque and vernacular examples, the Brutalist architects who dominated this section developed various new typologies for low-rise housing solutions that befitted the landscape and villages. James Stirling's proposal for a village extension builds on linear street patterns, while deploying local traditional methods of construction in response to the urgent need for immediate action. The proposal for so-called Fold Houses by Alison and Peter Smithson focuses on individual houses that match the local characteristics of climate, material and scale. In his plan, John Voelcker reconceptualizes the typology of peasants' homes.

Largely overlooked in the history of the CIAM and Team 10 is the rethinking of urban typologies by its members. Wilhelm Schütte presented an urban renewal project for the transformation of a Viennese block, thus creating new urban spaces in the inner city of the Austrian capital. Bill and Gill Howell, together with John Killick and John Partridge, proposed a scheme for London townhouses based on Georgian and Victorian examples. Aldo van Eyck's designs for playgrounds in Amsterdam are the best-known example of socio-urban regeneration ideas developed by CIAM and Team 10.

The American CIAM group GAI (Group for Architectural Investigation), including Team 10 member Blanche Lemco, proposed a scheme for suburban living that pays attention to a careful, cluster-like planning of the transitions between private, collective and public spaces.

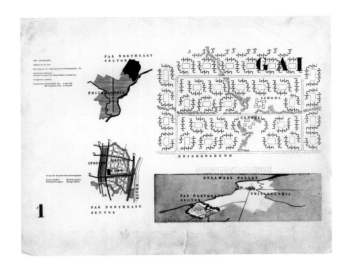 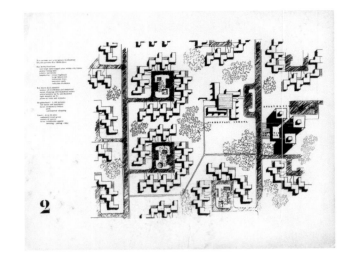

GAI
Robert Geddes, Romaldo
Giurgulo, Blanche Lemco,
George Qualls

'Habitat in the City', row
houses in a suburban area
of Philadelphia

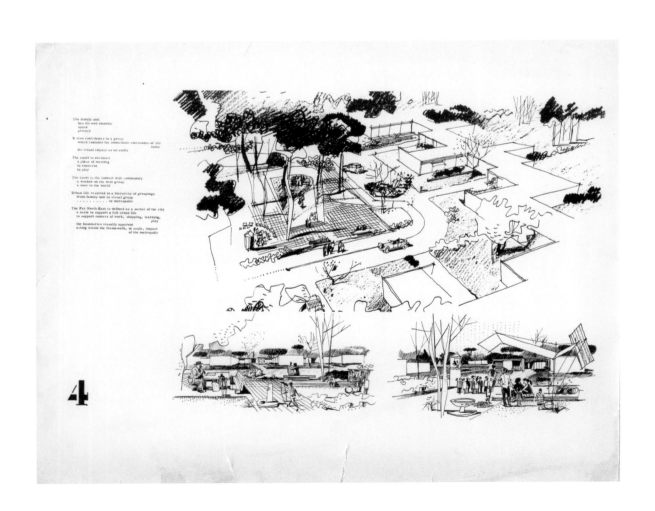

BLUTGASSE

CIAM-Austria
Wilhelm Schütte

**Urban renewal of the
inner city of Vienna**

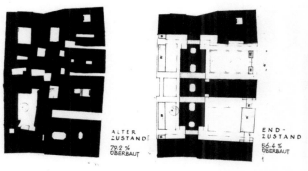

LOST IDENTITY

a city without the child's particular movement is a paradox. the child discovers its identity against all odds, damaged and damaging, in perpetual danger and incidental sunshine.

example: the child and the city

something the city
can absorb without
losing its remaining
identity; something
meant for the child
alone and not altogether
different from the incid-
ental things the child already adapts to its
imagination and vital-
ity; something care-
fully shaped and
judiciously placed
where there is still
some room.
on innumerable form-
less islands left over
by the road engineer
and demolition worker,
on empty plots. on
places better suited
to the child than the
public watering place.
70 such places have
been adapted in this city.

the playground as core and extension of the doorstep

de 8, Amsterdam
Aldo van Eyck

'Lost Identity', playgrounds
in Amsterdam

symbol towards
a partial
solution

2

hand in hand
with whatever
represents
imagination
unhusked
the child
survives
edged towards
the fringes
of our attention,
an emotional
and
unproductive
quantum.

snow! the child takes over. yet what it needs is

something far more permanent than snow.

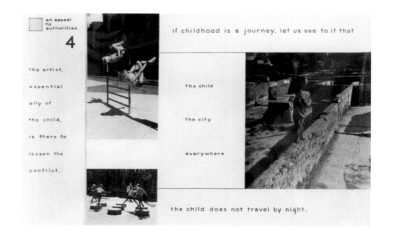

an appeal
to
authorities

4

the artist,

essential

ally of

the child,

is there to

lessen the

conflict.

if childhood is a journey, let us see to it that

the child

the city

everywhere

the child does not travel by night.

MARS GROUP
Alison and Peter-Smithson.

London.

Parent Community:
West Burton,
North Riding,
Yorkshire.
Location:England
Climate:temperate upland.
Population:350

fold
houses

VILLAGE.

1

TIREE: croft community. 1/Preservation of the terrain and herbage.
2/.a family of dwellings.

PROBLEM: TO INVENT A "TYPE HOUSE" FOR USE IN INFIL DEVELOPMENT IN A VILLAGE.

POROS: identical unit   used throughout (other island villages have their own unit) give an identity of coherence - like red apples on a tree.

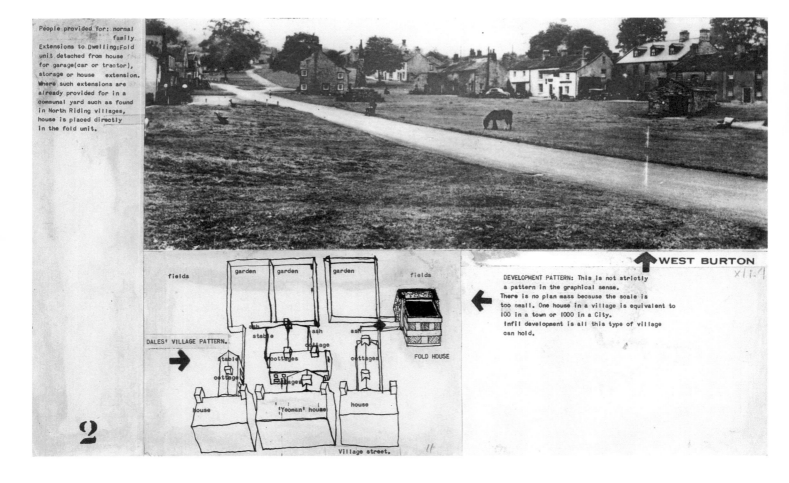

People provided for: normal
family
Extensions to Dwelling:Fold
unit detached from house
for garage(car or tractor),
storage or house extension.
Where such extensions are
already provided for in a
communal yard such as found
in North Riding villages,
house is placed directly
in the fold unit.

WEST BURTON

fields   garden   garden   garden   fields

DALES' VILLAGE PATTERN.

ash   stable   ash   ash

stable   cottage
cottage   cottages

cottage   cottages

house   'Yeoman' house   house

Village street.

FOLD HOUSE

DEVELOPMENT PATTERN: This is not strictly a pattern in the graphical sense.
There is no plan mass because the scale is too small. One house in a village is equivalent to 100 in a town or 1000 in a City.
Infil development is all this type of village can hold.

2

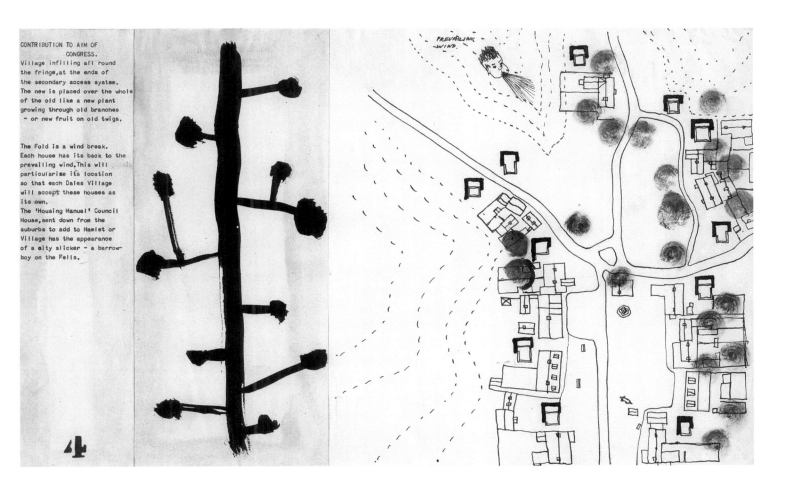

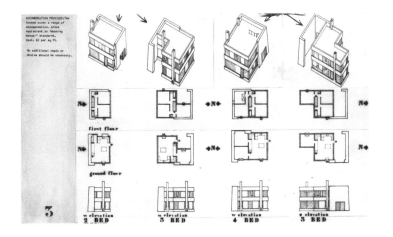

MARS Group
Alison and Peter Smithson

Fold Houses, infill
development project for
West Burton, Yorkshire

MARS Group
John Voelcker

Village Extension, project
for East Horsley, Surrey

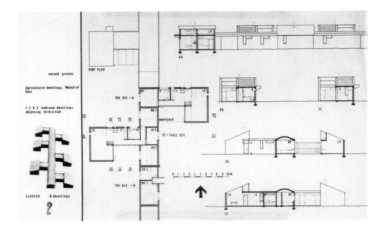

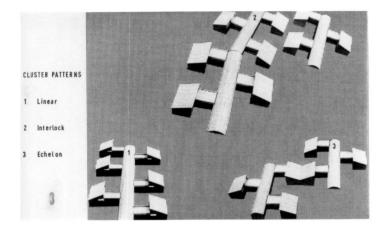

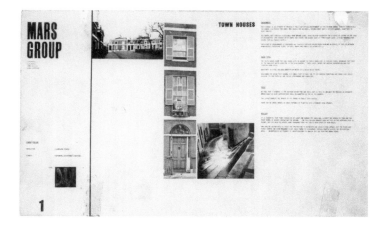

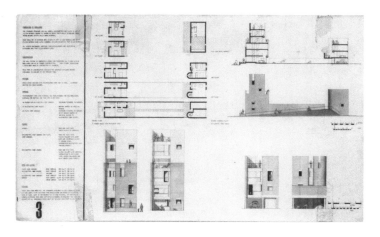

MARS Group
Bill and Gillian Howell,
John Killick, John Partridge

Town Houses, project for
London

M A R S G R O U P   B R I T A I N

THE FLOOR AREA PROVIDED IN THESE 1 TO 4
BEDROOM COTTAGES IS SLIGHTLY GREATER
THAN THAT OF URBAN FLATS WITH A COMPARA-
BLE NUMBER OF BEDROOMS, BUT CONSIDERABLY
LOWER THAN THAT REQUIRED BY THE MINISTRY
OF HOUSING FOR RURAL DEVELOPMENT.

LA SUPERFICIE PREVUE POUR CES MAISONS DE
1 A 4 CHAMBRES EST LEGEREMENT SUPERIEURE
A CELLE DE LA PLUPART DES APPARTEMENTS
URBAINS AYANT UN NOMBRE DE CHAMBRES COM-
PARABLE, MAIS CONSIDERABLEMENT INFERIEURE
A CELLE EXIGEE PAR LE MINISTRE DE LA
CONSTRUCTION DANS LES DEVELOPPEMENTS
RURAUX.

WEST WYCOMBE, Buckinghamshire (pop. 500). A roadside
village of the simplest form. Buildings of irregular heights and irregular
frontages facing straight on to the road with no garden intervening. Slight
variety of the middle of the street contains the village war memorial; while the
forking of the roads to the east, and the curving of the road to the west, contain
the village outstands. Brick, half-timber, weather-boarding,
plaster, colour wash; tiled roofs.

EXTENSIONS TO EXISTING VILLAGES IN ANY
PART OF BRITAIN; A SYSTEM TO COVER ALL
THE REQUIREMENTS OF LOW-COST HOUSING
ACCOMODATION RANGING FROM 1 TO 4 BED-
ROOMS.   AN ATTEMPT AT ORDER WITH INFI-
NITE VARIETY.   A FORM OF CONSTRUCTION
SUITABLE FOR LEVEL OR SLOPING GROUND,
(ADAPTABLE AS COTTAGES, SHOPS AND ANY
OTHER TYPE OF PREMISES REQUIRED IN A
VILLAGE).
LIGHT PENETRATES TO THE INTERIOR BET-
WEEN THE STRUCTURAL BAYS.   THE LONG
SIDES REMAIN WINDOWLESS EXCEPT WHERE
LIGHT IS ESSENTIAL; THEN SMALL OPENINGS
PUNCTUATE THE STRUCTURAL WALLS WHERE
REQUIRED.

ARCHITECT JAMES STIRLING. AUG. 1955.

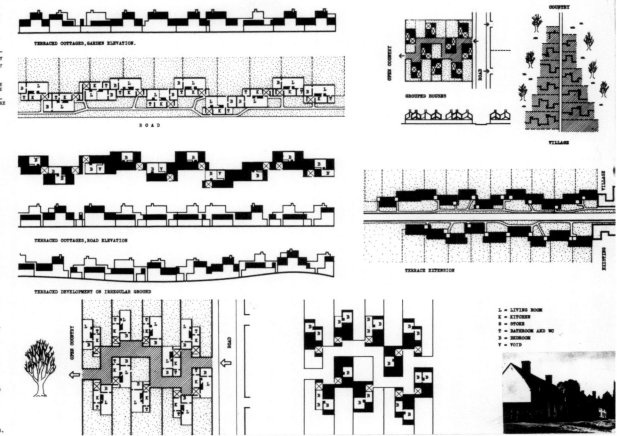

TERRACED COTTAGES, GARDEN ELEVATION.

ROAD

TERRACED COTTAGES, ROAD ELEVATION

TERRACED DEVELOPMENT ON IRREGULAR GROUND

GROUPED HOUSES

COUNTRY

ROAD

VILLAGE

TERRACE EXTENSION

OPEN COUNTRY

ROAD

L = LIVING ROOM
K = KITCHEN
S = STORE
T = BATHROOM AND WC
B = BEDROOM
V = VOID

C I A M X.   V I L L A G E

M A R S G R O U P   B R I T A I N

THE FORM OF THE ENGLISH VILLAGE HAS NOT
CHANGED IN THE LAST 400 YEARS AND HAS
HARDLY BEEN AFFECTED BY THE INDUSTRIAL
REVOLUTION.   HOUSING EXTENSIONS ARE RE-
QUIRED MAINLY TO PROVIDE FOR THE GROWTH
IN POPULATION DUE TO AN INCREASE IN LOCAL
TRADE AND AGRICULTURE, AND FOR THE TEN-
DENCY OF VILLAGES TO BECOME THE DORMITO-
RIES OF EXPANDING TOWNS.
THE BASIC FORM OF THE ENGLISH VILLAGE
CONSISTS OF BUILDINGS OF IRREGULAR HEIGHTS
AND FRONTAGES SPREADING ALONG EITHER SIDE
OF A THROUGH ROAD.   THE RARER VARIATION
OF THE ROAD-SIDE VILLAGE IS THE SQUARED
LAY-OUT CENTERED ON THE 'GREEN', OFTEN A
PLOT OF GRASSLAND WITH ONE EDGE ON THE
THROUGH ROAD.

AN ENGLISH VILLAGE.

LE SCHEMA DU VILLAGE ANGLAIS N'A GUERE
CHANGE PENDANT LES QUATRE DERNIERS SIECLES
ET S'EST A PEINE RESSENTI DE LA REVOLUTION
INDUSTRIELLE.   LE DEVELOPPEMENT DE
L'HABITATION EST DU PRINCIPALEMENT A UN
ACCROISSEMENT DE LA POPULATION PROVENANT
D'UNE HAUSSE DANS LE COMMERCE ET L'AGRI-
CULTURE LOCALE ET AUSSI A CETTE TENDANCE
QU'ONT LES VILLAGES A DEVENIR LES DORTOIRS
DES VILLES CROISSANTES.
SCHEMA DE BASE DU VILLAGE ANGLAIS: MAISONS
DE HAUTEURS ET DE FACADES IRREGULIERES
S'ETALANT DE PART ET D'AUTRE D'UNE ROUTE
TRANSVERSALE.   VARIANTE ASSEZ RARE: LE
PLAN ORTHOGONAL CENTRE AUTOUR DE LA
COMMUNE, EN GENERAL UNE ETENDUE DE GAZON
DONT UN COTE BORDE LA ROUTE TRANSVERSALE.

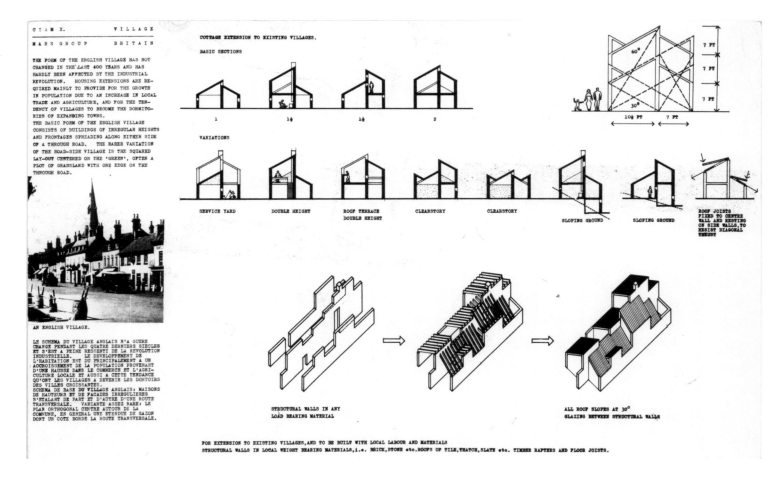

COTTAGE EXTENSION TO EXISTING VILLAGES.
BASIC SECTIONS

1   1½   1½   2

7 FT
7 FT
7 FT

60°   30°

10½ FT   7 FT

VARIATIONS

SERVICE YARD   DOUBLE HEIGHT   ROOF TERRACE DOUBLE HEIGHT   CLEARSTORY   CLEARSTORY   SLOPING GROUND   SLOPING GROUND   ROOF JOISTS FIXED TO CENTRE WALL AND RESTING ON SIDE WALLS, TO RESIST DIAGONAL THRUST

STRUCTURAL WALLS IN ANY
LOAD BEARING MATERIAL

ALL ROOF SLOPES AT 30°
GLAZING BETWEEN STRUCTURAL WALLS

FOR EXTENSION TO EXISTING VILLAGES, AND TO BE BUILT WITH LOCAL LABOUR AND MATERIALS
STRUCTURAL WALLS IN LOCAL WEIGHT BEARING MATERIALS, i.e. BRICK, STONE etc. ROOFS OF TILE, THATCH, SLATE etc. TIMBER RAFTERS AND FLOOR JOISTS.

Social Spaces

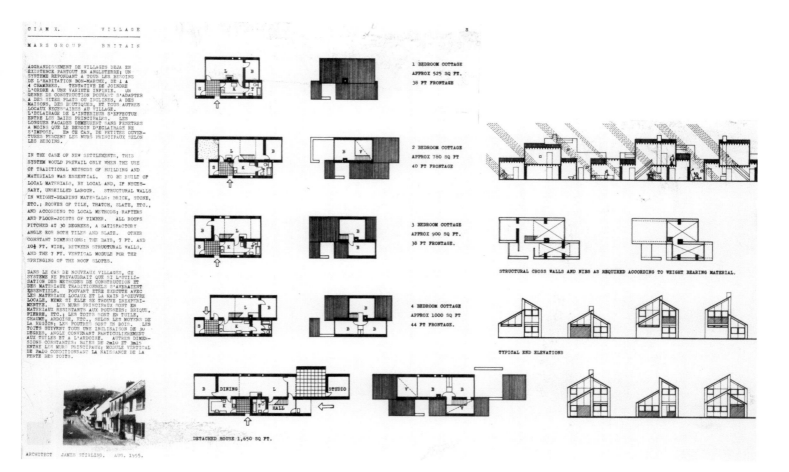

AGGRANDISSEMENT DE VILLAGES DEJA EN
EXISTENCE PARTOUT EN ANGLETERRE; UN
SYSTEME REPONDANT A TOUS LES BESOINS
DE L'HABITATION BON-MARCHE, DE 1 A
4 CHAMBRES. TENTATIVE DE JOINDRE
L'ORDRE A UNE VARIETE INFINIE. UN
GENRE DE CONSTRUCTION POUVANT S'ADAPTER
A DES SITES PLATS OU INCLINES, A DES
MAISONS, DES BOUTIQUES, ET TOUS AUTRES
LOCAUX NECESSAIRES AU VILLAGE.
L'ECLAIRAGE DE L'INTERIEUR S'EFFECTUE
ENTRE LES BAIES PRINCIPALES. LES
LONGUES FACADES DEMEURENT SANS FENETRES
A MOINS QUE LE BESOIN D'ECLAIRAGE NE
S'IMPOSE. EN CE CAS, DE PETITES OUVER-
TURES PERCENT LES MURS PRINCIPAUX SELON
LES BESOINS.

IN THE CASE OF NEW SETTLEMENTS, THIS
SYSTEM WOULD PREVAIL ONLY WHEN THE USE
OF TRADITIONAL METHODS OF BUILDING AND
MATERIALS WAS ESSENTIAL. TO BE BUILT OF
LOCAL MATERIALS, BY LOCAL AND, IF NECES-
SARY, UNSKILLED LABOUR. STRUCTURAL WALLS
IN WEIGHT-BEARING MATERIALS: BRICK, STONE,
ETC.; ROOVES OF TILE, THATCH, SLATE, ETC.,
AND ACCORDING TO LOCAL METHODS; RAFTERS
AND FLOOR-JOISTS OF TIMBER. ALL ROOFS
PITCHED AT 30 DEGREES, A SATISFACTORY
ANGLE ROR BOTH TILES AND SLATE. OTHER
CONSTANT DIMENSIONS: THE BAYS, 7 FT. AND
10½ FT. WIDE, BETWEEN STRUCTURAL WALLS,
AND THE 7 FT. VERTICAL MODULE FOR THE
SPRINGING OF THE ROOF SLOPES.

DANS LE CAS DE NOUVEAUX VILLAGES, CE
SYSTEME NE PREVAUDRAIT QUE SI L'UTILI-
SATION DES METHODES DE CONSTRUCTION ET
DES MATERIAUX TRADITIONNELS S'AVERAIENT
ESSENTIELS. POUVANT ETRE EXECUTE AVEC
LES MATERIAUX LOCAUX ET LA MAIN D'OEUVRE
LOCALE, MEME SI ELLE SE TROUVE INEXPERI-
MENTEE. LES MURS PRINCIPAUX SONT EN
MATERIAUX RESISTANTS AUX POUSSEES: BRIQUE,
PIERRE, ETC.; LES TOITS SONT EN TUILE,
CHAUME, ARDOISE, ETC., SELON LES MOYENS DE
LA REGION; LES POUTRES SONT EN BOIS. LES
TOITS SUIVENT TOUS UNE INCLINAISON DE 30
DEGRES, ANGLE CONVENANT PARTICULIEREMENT
AUX TUILES ET A L'ARDOISE. AUTRES DIMEN-
SIONS CONSTANTES: BAIES DE 2m10 ET 3m15
ENTRE LES MURS PRINCIPAUX; MODULE VERTICAL
DE 2m10 CONDITIONNANT LA NAISSANCE DE LA
PENTE DES TOITS.

ARCHITECT JAMES STIRLING, AVL. 1955.

1 BEDROOM COTTAGE
APPROX 525 SQ FT.
38 FT FRONTAGE

2 BEDROOM COTTAGE
APPROX 780 SQ FT
40 FT FRONTAGE

3 BEDROOM COTTAGE
APPROX 900 SQ FT.
38 FT FRONTAGE.

4 BEDROOM COTTAGE
APPROX 1000 SQ FT
44 FT FRONTAGE.

STRUCTURAL CROSS WALLS AND NIBS AS REQUIRED ACCORDING TO WEIGHT BEARING MATERIAL.

TYPICAL END ELEVATIONS

DETACHED HOUSE 1,650 SQ FT.

MARS Group
James Stirling

**Cottage extension to
existing villages, project
for West Wycombe,
Buckinghamshire, 1955**

LANDSCAPE INTERVENTIONS

Presentations at CIAM 10 – Meso-scale

A series of projects presented at Dubrovnik display careful attention to the existing, environmental, geographical and ecological conditions in which the designs were to be embedded. Rather than a functionalist tabula rasa approach, the new, modern housing schemes were considered as interventions in an existing milieu, with its own qualities and values.

The Portuguese submission by the CIAM Porto group shows such a careful analysis of the topographical and economic situation of a rural village in the mountainous north of the then underdeveloped country. The architects sought to achieve a precarious balance between renewal and continuity of social habits and the amelioration of the poor housing conditions of the local inhabitants. A modest housing typology was created from local materials in combination with prefab concrete elements. Over the years, and in line with evolving needs, these houses could be transformed and extended by the inhabitants themselves.

Geir Grung, Arne Korsmo and visual artist Gunnar Gundersen brought a sculptural housing scheme to Dubrovnik on behalf of the Norwegian PAGON (Progressive Architects Group Oslo Norway). One panel depicts the variety of relations between architecture, settlements and the natural landscape while another shows a range of social situations. The design proposal sought to rebalance such reciprocities with a project that negotiated the topographical conditions of the site.

Romke Romke de Vries, a Dutch member of the Rotterdam CIAM chapter Opbouw, meticulously analysed the landscape conditions of the Dutch delta, also in relation to the local climate conditions and the sociocultural context. He did so by drawing a section through the flat Dutch landscape, from the coastal dune landscape to the polders, their canals, and the inner lakes and hill regions, while acknowledging soil qualities and typical vegetation patterns. The modern houses occupy the landscape in a subtle and flexible way.

In a similar spirit, the Smithsons proposed a typology of 'houses riding the landscape'. Their idea for Close Houses was meant to present an alternative to the generic kind of suburban housing that was springing up around the United Kingdom in those years. Instead, in their view strings of small-scale, low-rise houses around a collective, covered alley would enable a vernacular kind of occupation of the open English landscape in line with age-old building traditions.

Geir Grung : architects.
Arne Korsmo:
G. S. Gundersen: painter.

INFORMATION

THE PROBLEM IS
FOCUSED ON: RELATION
BUILDING AND NATURE,
FLEXIBILITY OF THE
HABITAT.

1.
On the first page we show
you humanity's natural
and simple understanding
of the home and the
relationship of one's
dwelling to nature.

In its industrial development Oslo has become
the migration center from
country to town.

The first picture
illustrates the farm and
the farmer's simple
understanding of living
in its relation ship to
nature as defined through
time into a form-expres-
sion and milieu of high
cultural quality.
In the same way the homes
of the fishermen, either
as a neighborhood, has
attained its quality through
milieu and structure just
as have the old patrician
homes with their sculptural architecture and their
relationship to nature and
garden. All these build-
ing belong to the landscape
whether they seem to slip
away or lay close to it.

The early city home was
a carée structure with
its chopped up and closed
inner rooms. This was a
proper solution at that
time within the then ex-
isting understanding of
building techniques. But
even these homes had a
dimension of scale and
space between street,
garden and the building.

Oslo like most cities has
gone through a shift from
tranquility and simplicity
to the speed, the typycally
hurried and economically
hazarded impression of
our age.

Earlier craftsmen, archi-
tects and building methods
were influenced by the
naturally slower tempo of
that time and building
developments were under-
standable within their
age. Our times are plagued
with problems involving
tempo and quality.
Variations of materials
and advanced techniques
do not give us a sense of

Landscape interventions

PAGON
Geir Grung, Arne Korsmo,
Gunnar Sigmund Gundersen

Project for Oslo, bringing
together housing and nature

MARS GROUP

Alison and Peter Smithson

London.

Parent Community:New Town
Location:England.
Climate:Temperate.
Population:40-60,000.

close
houses

TOWN.

1

Tents at Crimean War.

Water holes - Sahara.

Yard pattern - Holland.

IDENTIFICATION IMAGE.
These shew the possibilities
of free-moving linear arrangement of elements and the
aptness of the yard idea to
the human habitat.

PROBLEM: TO DEVELOPE A NEW

TYPE OF COVERED STREET

SUITABLE FOR A NEW TOWN.

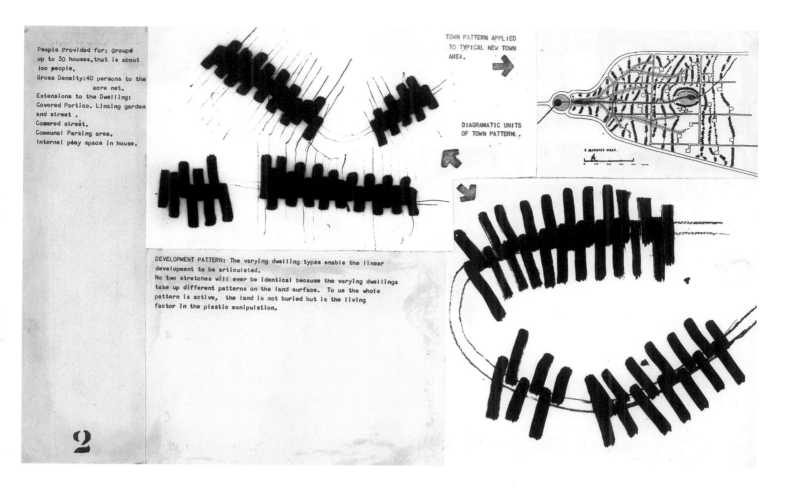

People provided for: Groups
up to 30 houses, that is about
100 people.
Gross Density: 40 persons to the
acre net.
Extensions to the Dwelling:
Covered Portico. Linking garden
and street.
Covered street.
Communal Parking area.
Internal play space in house.

DEVELOPMENT PATTERN: The varying dwelling types enable the linear
development to be articulated.
No two stretches will ever be identical because the varying dwellings
take up different patterns on the land surface. To us the whole
pattern is active, the land is not buried but is the living
factor in the plastic manipulation.

TOWN PATTERN APPLIED
TO TYPICAL NEW TOWN
AREA.

DIAGRAMATIC UNITS
OF TOWN PATTERN.

2

MARS Group
Alison and Peter Smithson

Close Houses, project for
a new type of covered street
for a New Town

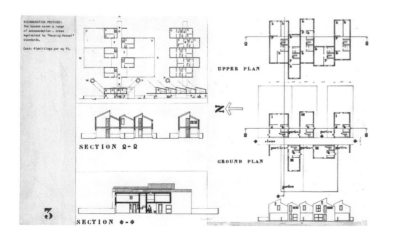

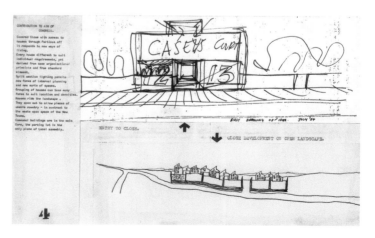

CIAM X

GROUPE CIAM PORTO
PORTUGAL

HABITAT RURAL

NOUVELLE COMMUNAUTE AGRICOLE

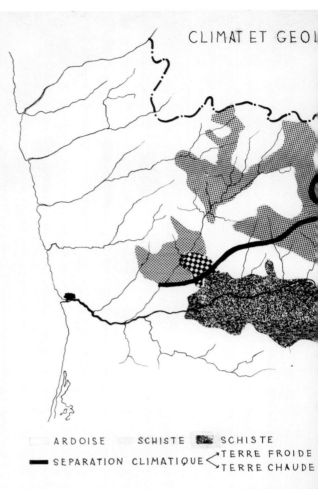

CLIMAT ET GEOL

ARDOISE   SCHISTE   ▨ SCHISTE

━━ SEPARATION CLIMATIQUE ⟨ TERRE FROIDE / TERRE CHAUDE

RELATIONS

RELATIONS ENTRE ELEMENTS REGIONAUX
ET CONTEMPORAINS / MOYENS D'EXPRES-
SION AU SUJET DE
    — USAGE DE TECHNIQUES TRADITIONEL
LES ET MATERIAUX LOCAUX
    — SATISFACTION DE VIEILLES HABITU
DES (MANIERES DE VIVRE) A TRAVERS LES
ACTUELLES POSSIBILITES DE CONSTRUCTION
    — CONSIDERATIONS CLIMATIQUES

———

LE PORTUGAL ETANT ENCORE UN
PAYS SURTOUT D'UN CARACTERE AGRICOLE

49		AGRICULTURE
28	▨	INDUSTRIE
23		ADMINISTRATION

ET EN CONSTITUANT LE CAS RURAL, COMME
C'EST VULGAIRE DANS TOUT LE MONDE, LA
DERNIERE PREOCUPATION DES RESPONSABLES/
EN VERIFIANT MEME QUE LA PREDOMINANCE DE
L'URBAIN SUR LE RURAL EST MANIFESTE ME
ME DANS LE CHAMP DE NOTRE ACTIVITE PRO
FESSIONELLE ET DOCTRINAIRE, LE CHOIX DU
THEME POUR LE PRESENT TRAVAIL S'EST BA
SÉ DANS L'ETUDE D'UN VILLAGE SITUE DANS
L'UNE DES REGIONS LES PLUS CARACTERIS
TIQUES, CONFORME AU PROJET (PANNEUX
2 ET 3)

———

LA REGION

"LOMBADA" AU N.E DE "BRAGANÇA",
REGION DE PLATEAU
TERRAIN DE SCHISTE ET ARDOISE
CULTURES DE MONTAGNE
CLIMAT "TERRE FROIDE" ("TERRA FRIA")

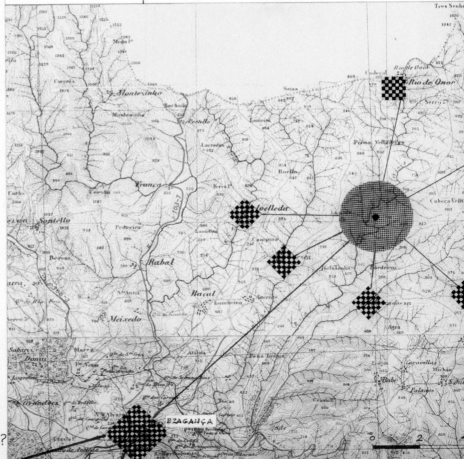

1 POURQUOI MANTENIR, PAR
PARESSE OU NÉGLIGENCE,
LE DÉCLASSEMENT DU PAYSAN?
L.C.

Landscape interventions

54

CULTURES DE MONTAGNE AVEC MAQUIS   CULTURES D'ARBRES ET D'ARBRI —
SSEAUX   TRANSITION   CULTURES ARROSÉES   CULTURES DE MONTAGNE
AVEC ÉLEVAGE   SAIGLE +BLÉ

CIAM Porto
Octávio Lixa Filgueiras,
Fernando Távora, Alfredo
Viana de Lima; together
with Arnaldo Araújo,
Carlos Carvalho Dias

'Rural Habitat: New
Agricultural Community'
in Lombada, Portugal

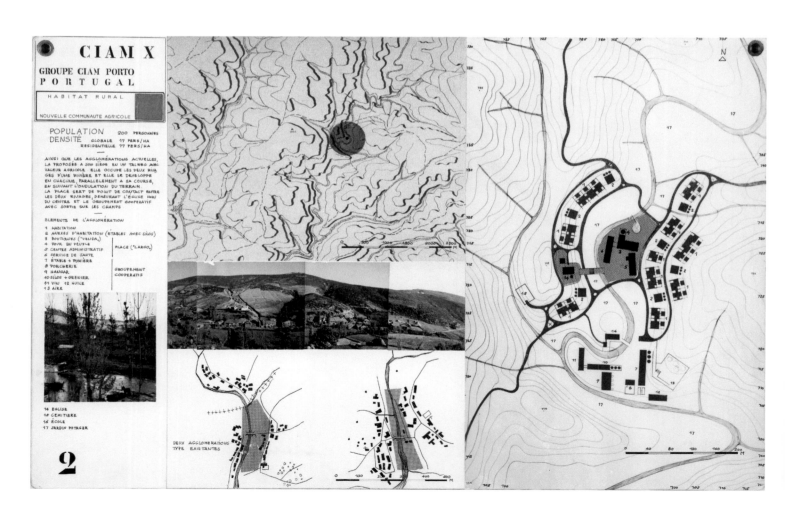

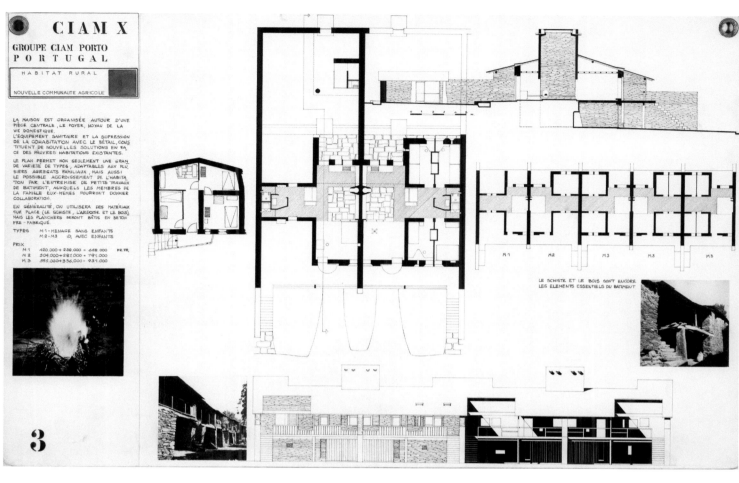

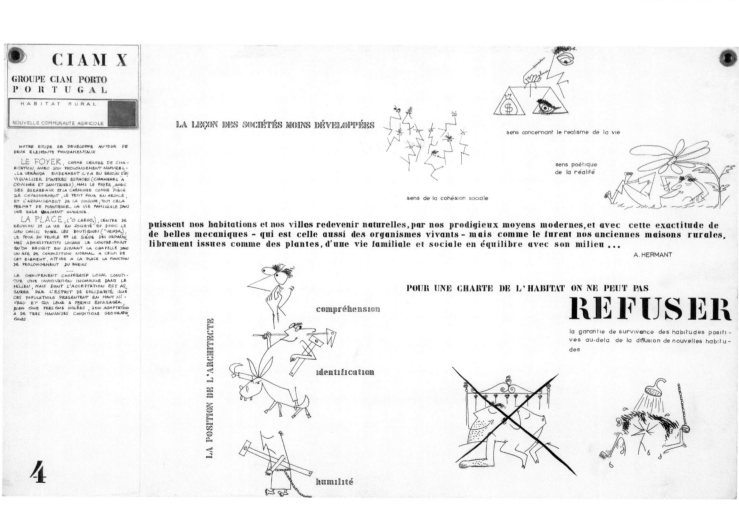

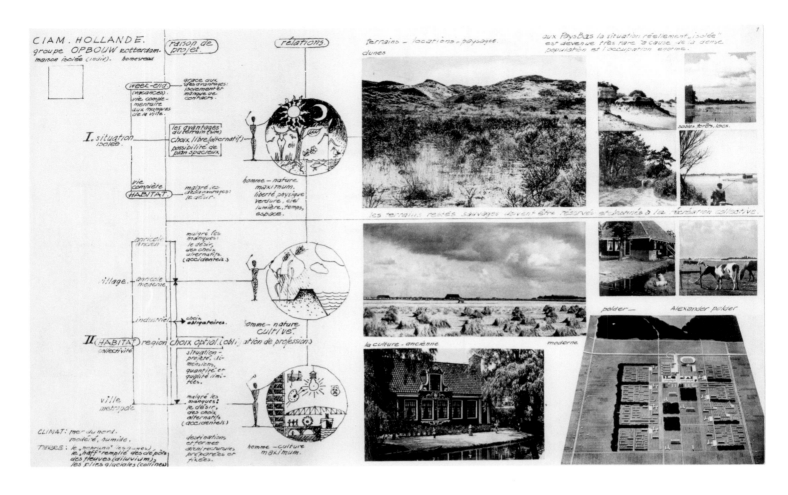

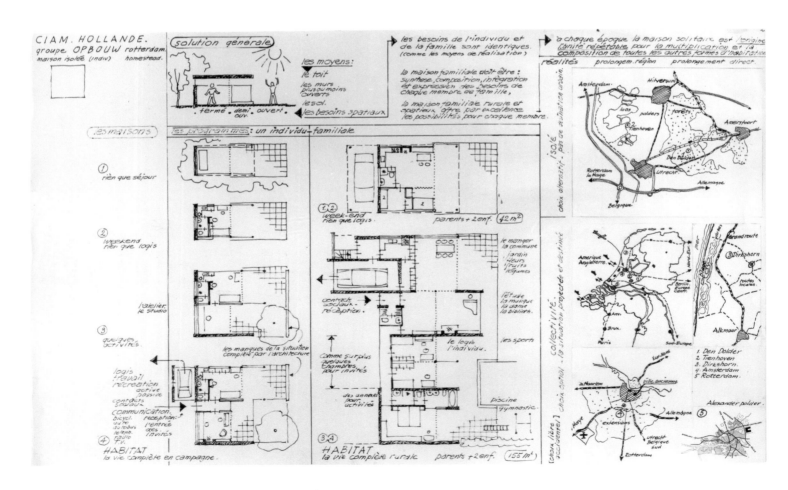

Landscape interventions

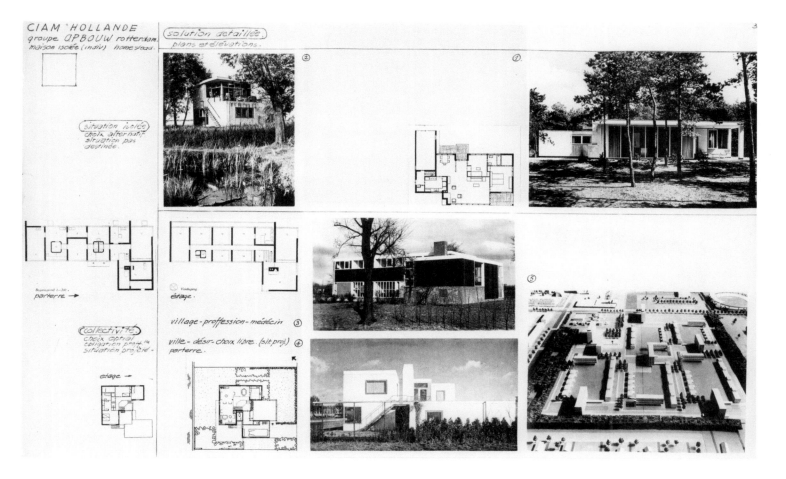

**CIAM Holland, Opbouw
Group Rotterdam**
Romke Romke de Vries

Rationale, principles
and design for an individual
homestead in Holland

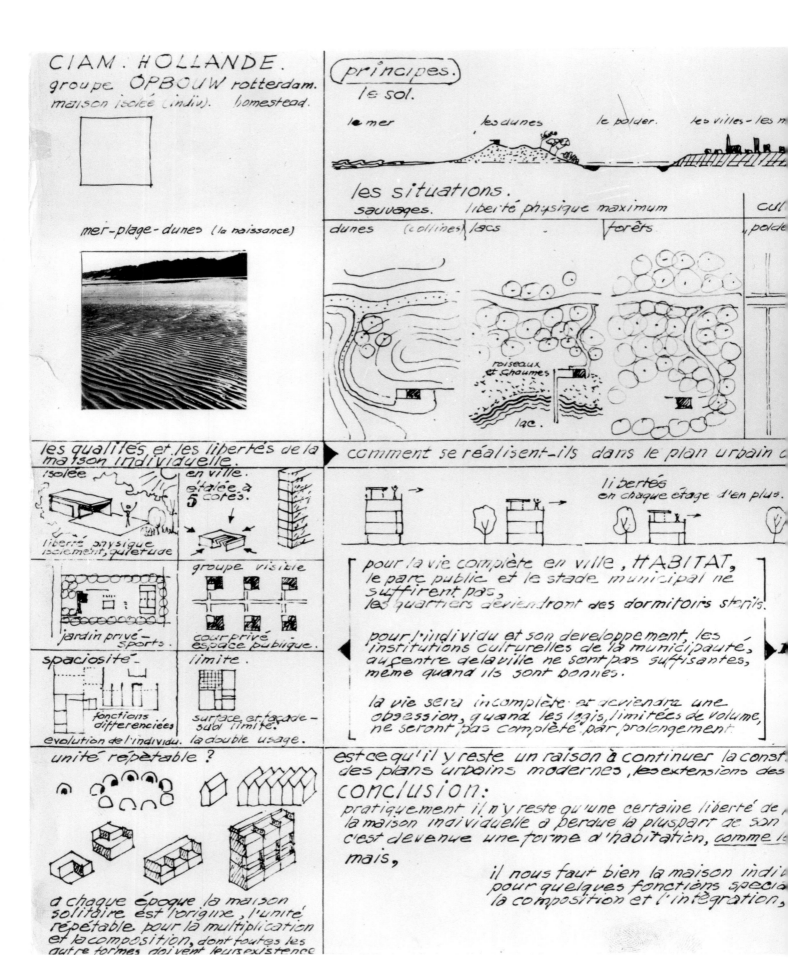

CIAM. HOLLANDE.

groupe OPBOUW rotterdam.

maison isolée (indiv). homestead.

mer-plage-dunes (la naissance)

le mer   les dunes   le polder.   les villes - les m

les situations.

sauvages.   liberté physique maximum   cul

dunes   (collines) lacs   forêts.   polde

roiseaux
et chaumes

lac.

les qualités et les libertés de la maison individuelle.

comment se réalisent-ils dans le plan urbain a

isolée   en ville.
                          étalée à
                          5 côtés.

liberté physique
isolement, quiétude

libertés
en chaque étage d'en plus.

groupe visible

jardin privé - sports.   cour privé
                            espace publique.

pour la vie complète en ville, HABITAT,
le parc public et le stade municipal ne
suffirent pas,
les quartiers deviendront des dormitoirs stériles.

spaciosité -   limite.

fonctions
différenciées
évolution de l'individu.

surface et façade -
subl limité.
la double usage.

pour l'individu et son developpement, les
institutions culturelles de la municipauté,
au centre de la ville ne sont pas suffisantes,
même quand ils sont bonnes.

la vie sera incomplète et deviendra une
obsession, quand les logis, limitées de volume,
ne seront pas complété par prolongement.

unité répétable ?

a chaque époque la maison
solitaire est l'origine, l'unité
répétable pour la multiplication
et la composition, dont toutes les
autres formes doivent leur existence

est ce qu'il y reste un raison à continuer la const.
des plans urbains modernes, les extensions des

conclusion:

pratiquement il n'y reste qu'une certaine liberté de,
la maison individuelle a perdue la pluspart de son
c'est devenue une forme d'habitation, comme l
mais,

il nous faut bien la maison indiv
pour quelques fonctions spécia
la composition et l'intégration,

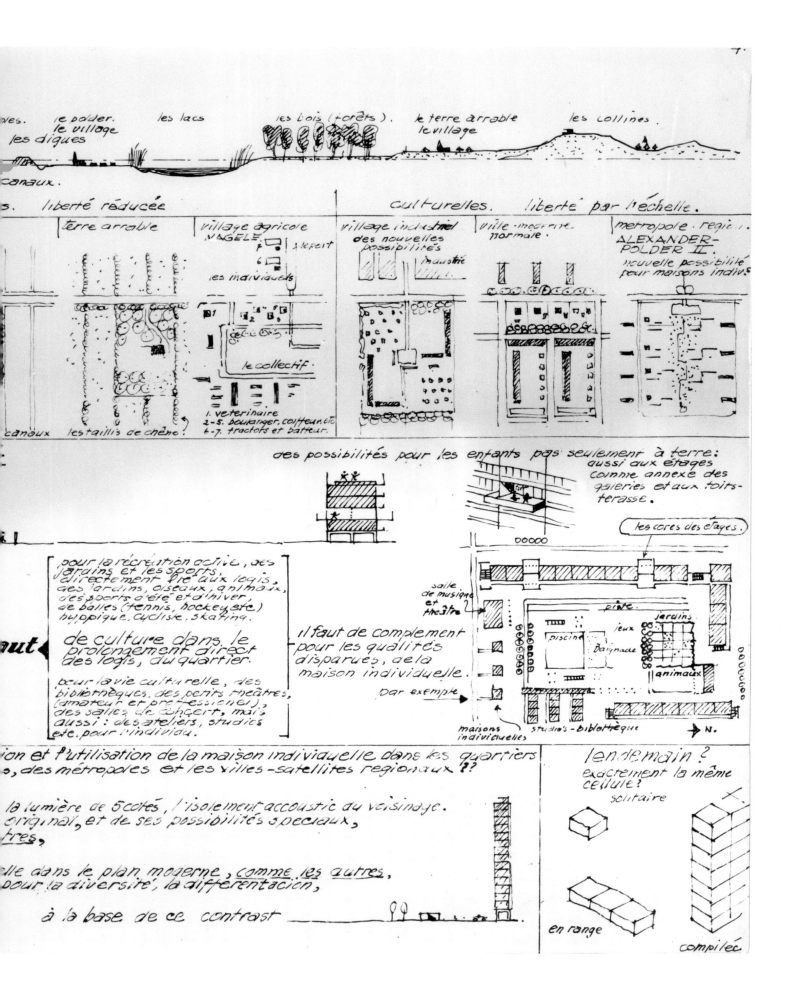

TOTALITIES

Presentations at CIAM 10 – Macro-scale

A number of presentations from CIAM 10 operated on the regional scale with schemes that aimed at providing housing for tens, or even hundreds of thousands of people in varying degrees of autonomy with regard to the landscape in which they were to be situated. Besides a holistic approach, these projects display an aesthetic ambition to translate the ideals of habitat into an abstracted architectural language in confrontation with the landscape. An almost cosmological dimension is achieved here.

From the projects that survive in the archive, the Dutch contributions stand out in this respect, in line with the strong tradition of planning and centuries of experience with creating new land through polders. Jaap Bakema, together with the Rotterdam CIAM-group Opbouw, presented his ongoing design research into whole new districts and new towns, from Pendrecht to Alexanderpolder in Rotterdam. He undertook this work together with Lotte Stam-Beese, who – after her breakup with Mart Stam – would find employment as chief urban designer for the City of Rotterdam, and with Jan Stokla, one of the most talented housing designers at the firm of Van den Broek and Bakema.

The Rotterdam office of Oyevaar and Stolle proposed a socialist settlement for industry workers as an illustration of the Alexanderpolder scheme of Opbouw. The rationalist logic of both the polder layout and mass housing is translated into an aesthetic of infinitely extending grids to achieve the desired interrelationships between people and built environment within the hermetic confines of the project.

Besides his playgrounds, Aldo van Eyck presented a second project: the polder village of Nagele, which had been a collective effort by architects from the Dutch CIAM and its two Amsterdam and Rotterdam branches. To house the community of field labourers the Nagele design proposes the creation of a protected area within the vast, wind-swept expansion of the new Noordoostpolder. A structuralist configuration of interconnected housing neighbourhoods and open spaces characterizes the planning from the smallest scale level up to the whole settlement.

Reima Pietilä of the Finnish PTAH (Progrès, Téchnique, Architecture Helsinki) group showed a proposal for an underground industry settlement to be located beyond the arctic circle. The extreme climate conditions led to the developments of massive subterraneous units that would be self-contained and possess a functional organization of a 'planetaric character'. The units were to accommodate from a hundred thousand people up to a million. The poetic quality of Pietilä's proposal is derived from the combination of a most diagrammatic language of abstract proportions and spatial relations with the geological landscape formations of the Finnish arctic landscape.

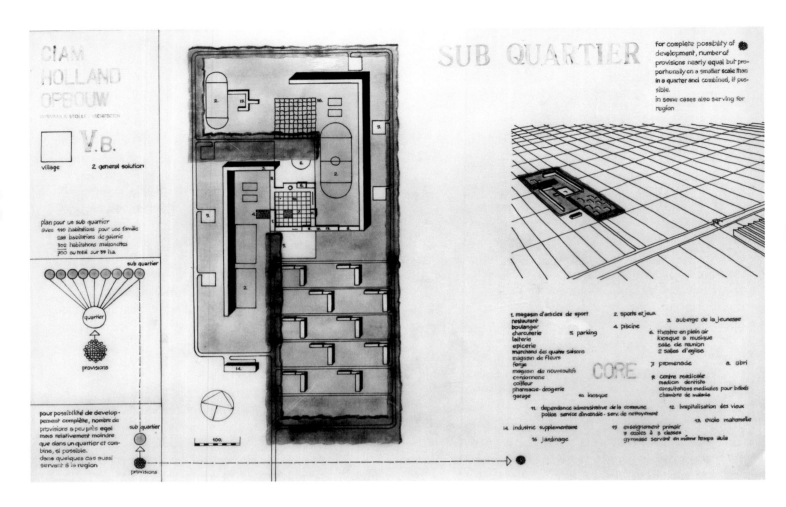

**CIAM Holland, Opbouw
Group Rotterdam**
Arnold Oyevaar and
Hein Stolle

Plan for an isolated
neighbourhood

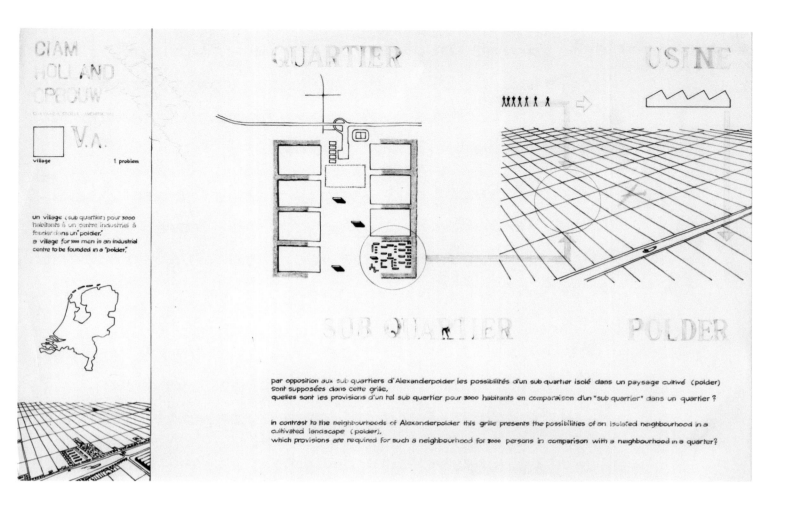

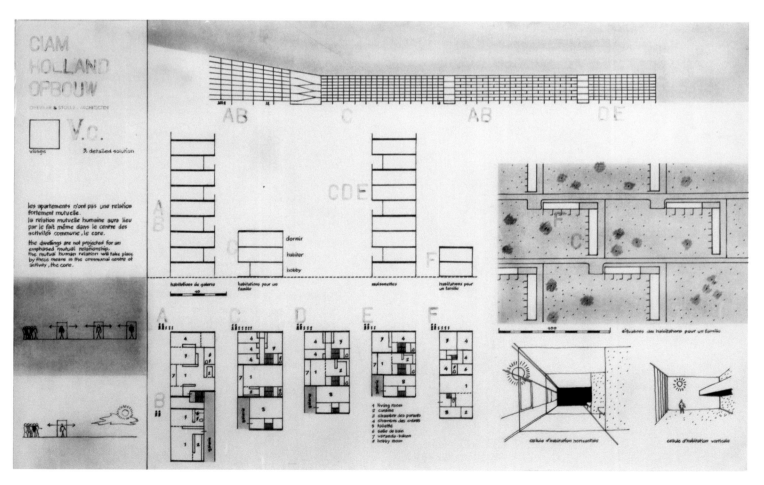

CIAM HOLLANDE GROUPE OPBOUW

la ville

A4

één van de noodzakelijke voorwaarden voor „habitat" is de expressie van samenhang (core) tussen de verschillende woonvormen in herhaalbare wooneenheden (visual groups)

une des conditions indispensables pour habitat c'est l'expression d'interrelation (core) entre les différentes formes de logis en unités d'habitation répétantes (visual groups)

the expression of the interrelationship (core) of the various dwellingtypes in repetable units (visual groups) is one of the indispensable conditions for „habitat"

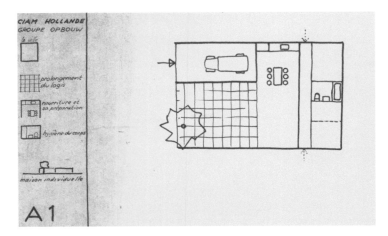

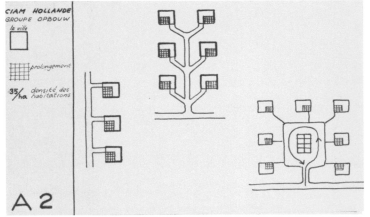

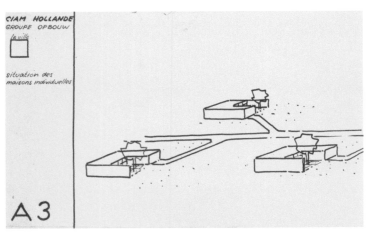

CIAM Holland, Opbouw Group Rotterdam
Jaap Bakema and Jan Stokla

Grids for various dwelling types in visual groups for Alexanderpolder, prepared for the CIAM meeting in La Sarraz (1955)

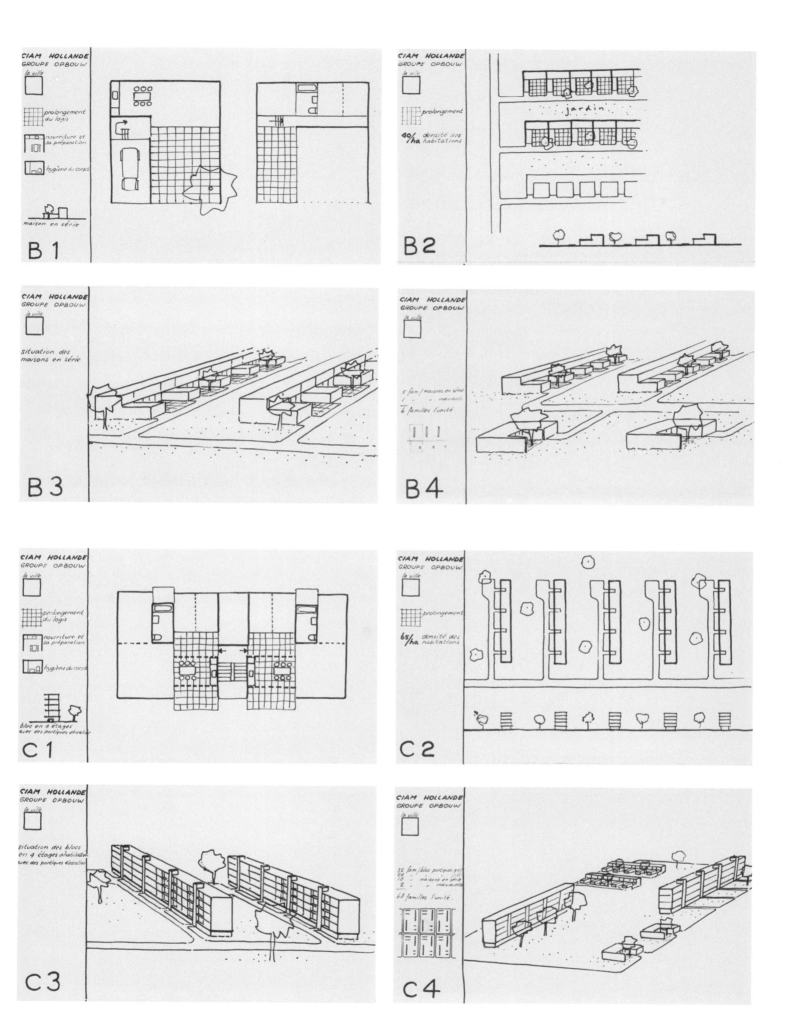

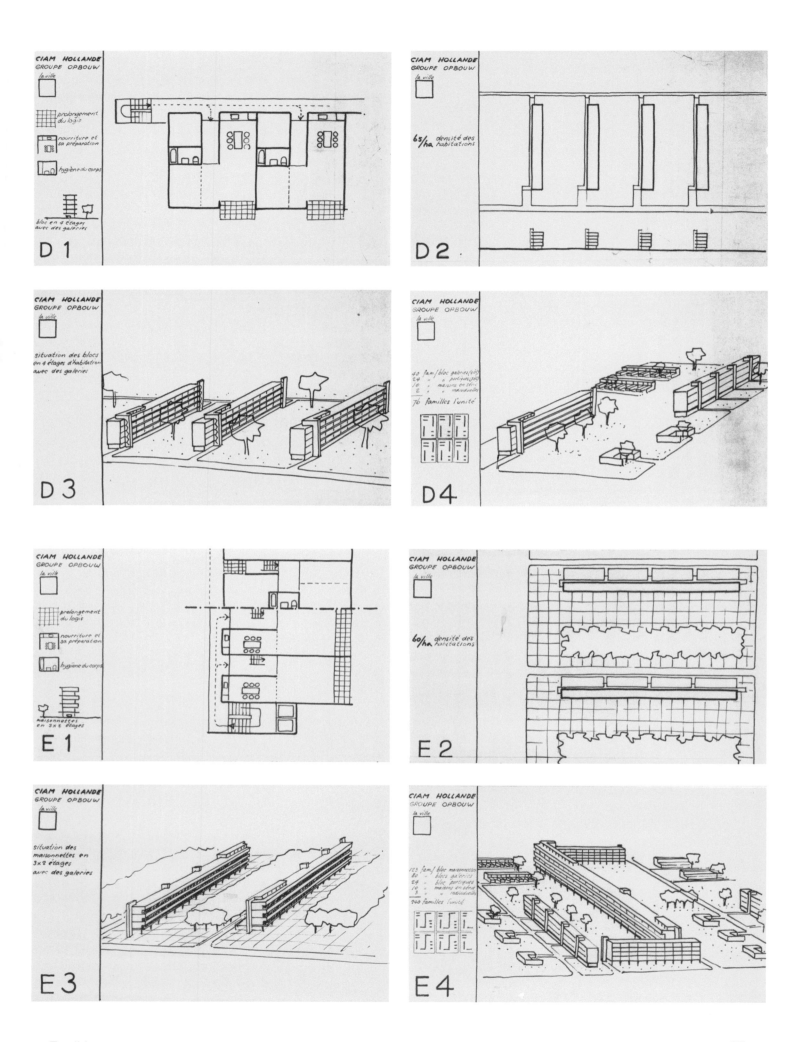

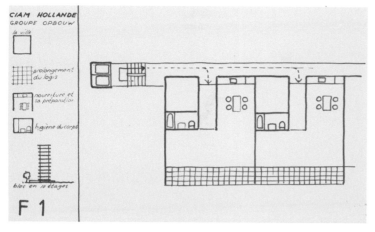

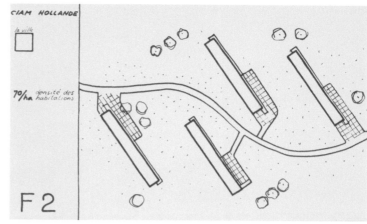

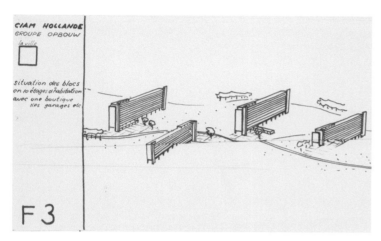

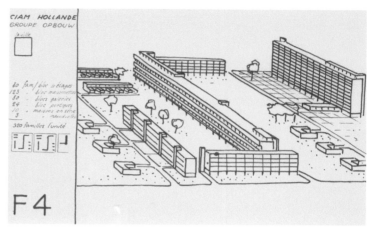

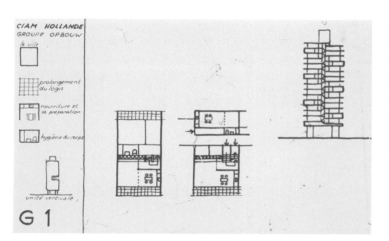

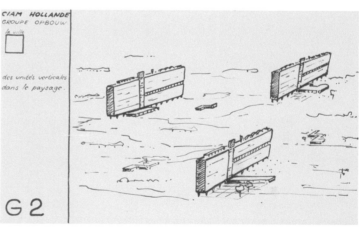

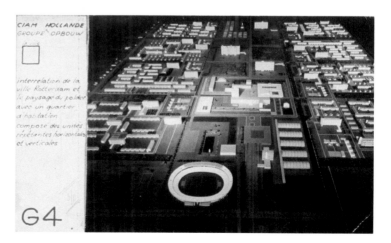

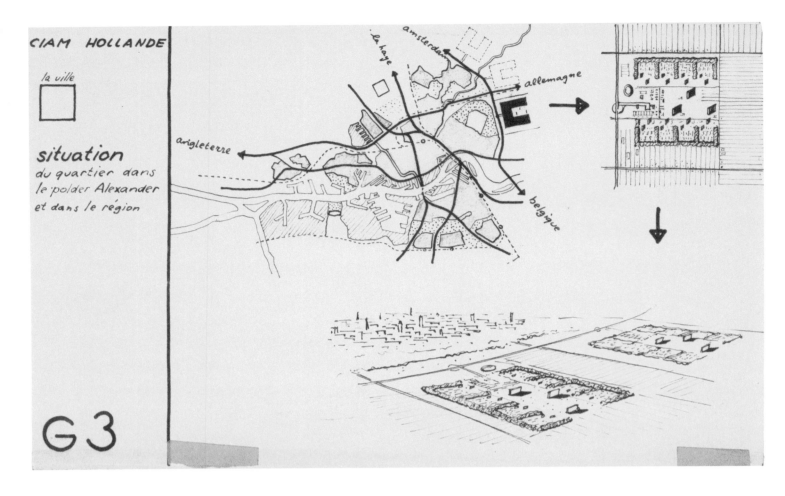

CIAM HOLLANDE

la ville

situation
du quartier dans
le polder Alexander
et dans le région

amsterdam

la haye

allemagne

angleterre

belgique

G3

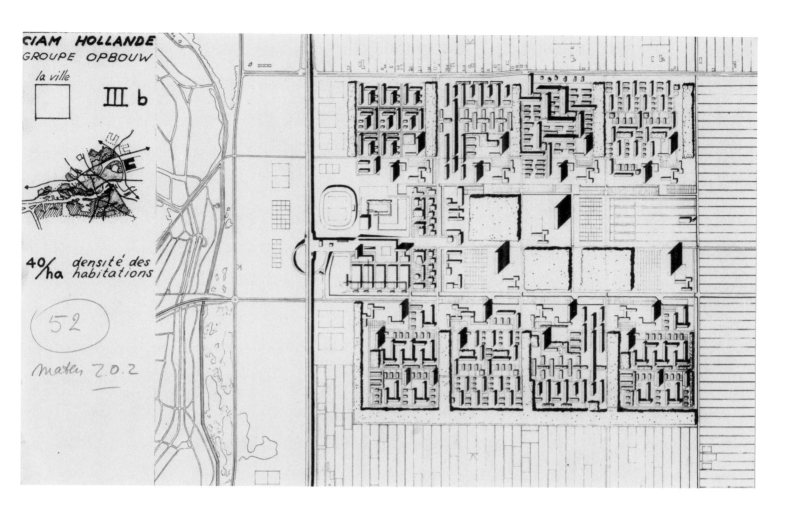

CIAM Holland,
Opbouw Group Rotterdam
Jaap Bakema and Jan Stokla

Part of a set of three grids for
Alexanderpolder, Rotterdam,
1956

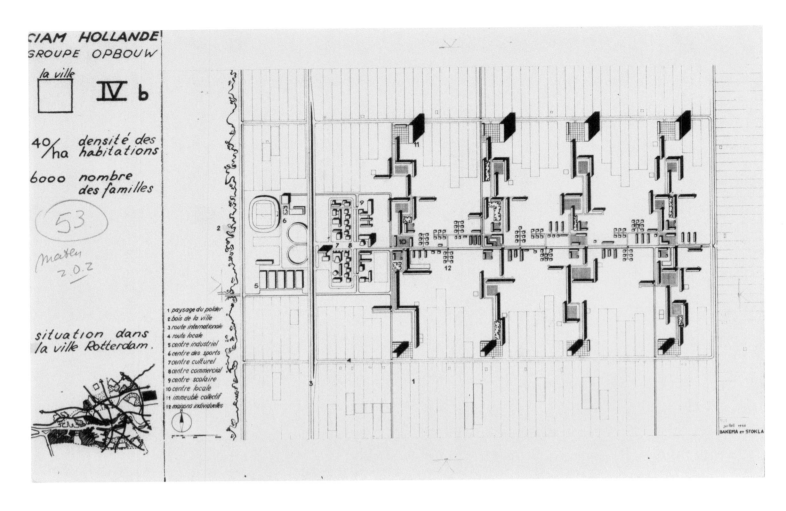

CIAM HOLLANDE
GROUPE OPBOUW

la ville

IV b

40/ha densité des habitations

6000 nombre des familles

53

maten 2.0.2

situation dans la ville Rotterdam.

1 paysage du polder
2 bois de la ville
3 route internationale
4 route locale
5 centre industriel
6 centre des sports
7 centre culturel
8 centre commercial
9 centre scolaire
10 centre locale
11 immeuble collectif
12 maisons individuelles

**CIAM Holland, Opbouw
Group Rotterdam**
Jaap Bakema and Jan Stokla

Part of a set of three grids for
Alexanderpolder, Rotterdam,
1956

Totalities

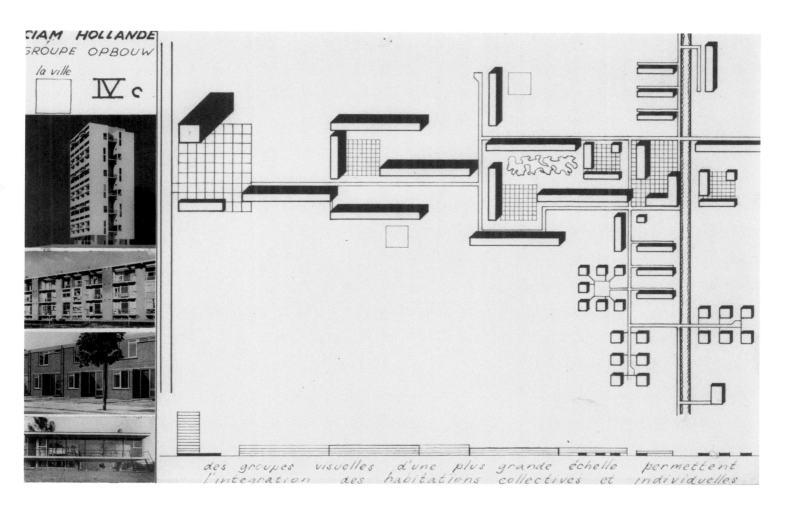

des groupes visuelles d'une plus grande échelle permettent
l'intégration des habitations collectives et individuelles

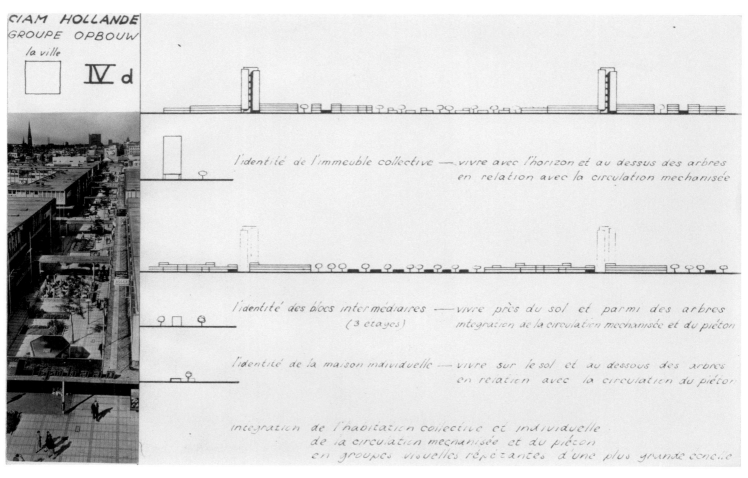

l'identité de l'immeuble collective — vivre avec l'horizon et au dessus des arbres
en relation avec la circulation mechanisée

l'identité des blocs intermédiaires — vivre près du sol et parmi des arbres
(3 étages)   intégration de la circulation mechanisé et du piéton

l'identité de la maison individuelle — vivre sur le sol et au dessous des arbres
en relation avec la circulation du piéton

intégration de l'habitation collective et individuelle
de la circulation mechanisée et du piéton
en groupes visuelles répétantes d'une plus grande échelle

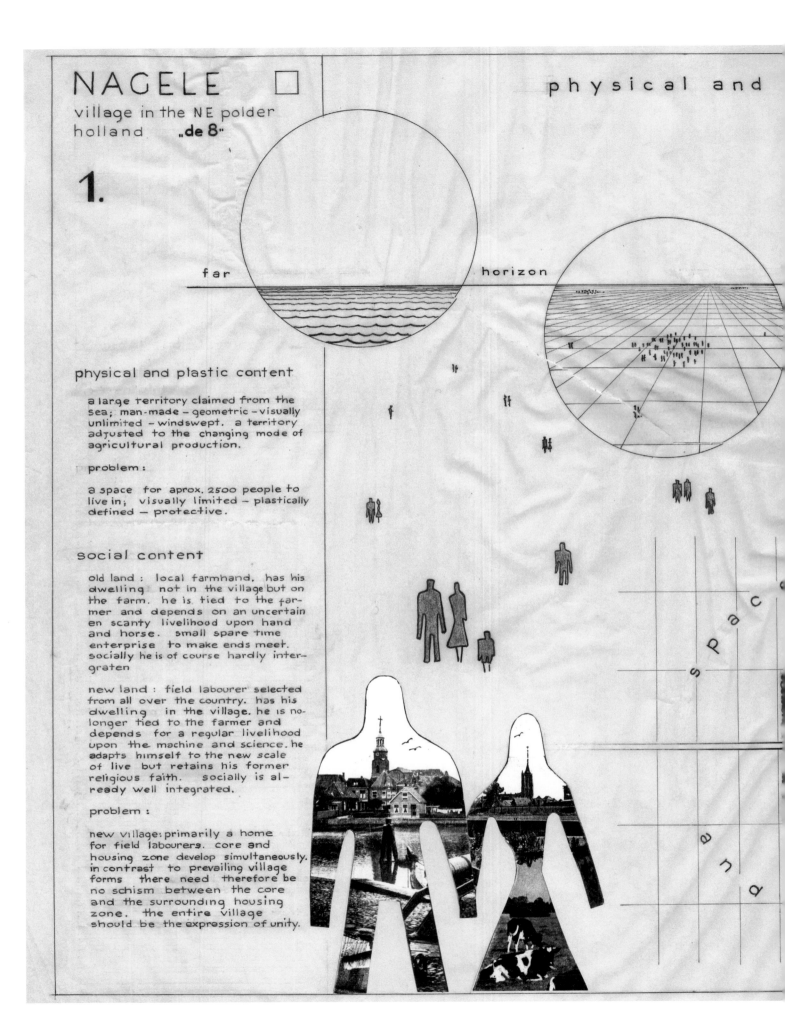

NAGELE □

village in the NE polder
holland "de 8"

1.

far   horizon

physical and plastic content

a large territory claimed from the
sea; man-made – geometric – visually
unlimited – windswept. a territory
adjusted to the changing mode of
agricultural production.

problem :

a space for aprox. 2500 people to
live in; visually limited – plastically
defined – protective.

social content

old land : local farmhand, has his
dwelling not in the village but on
the farm. he is tied to the farmer and depends on an uncertain
en scanty livelihood upon hand
and horse. small spare time
enterprise to make ends meet.
socially he is of course hardly inter-
graten

new land : field labourer selected
from all over the country. has his
dwelling in the village. he is no-
longer tied to the farmer and
depends for a regular livelihood
upon the machine and science. he
adapts himself to the new scale
of live but retains his former
religious faith. socially is already well integrated.

problem :

new village: primarily a home
for field labourers. core and
housing zone develop simultaneously.
in contrast to prevailing village
forms there need therefore be
no schism between the core
and the surrounding housing
zone. the entire village
should be the expression of unity.

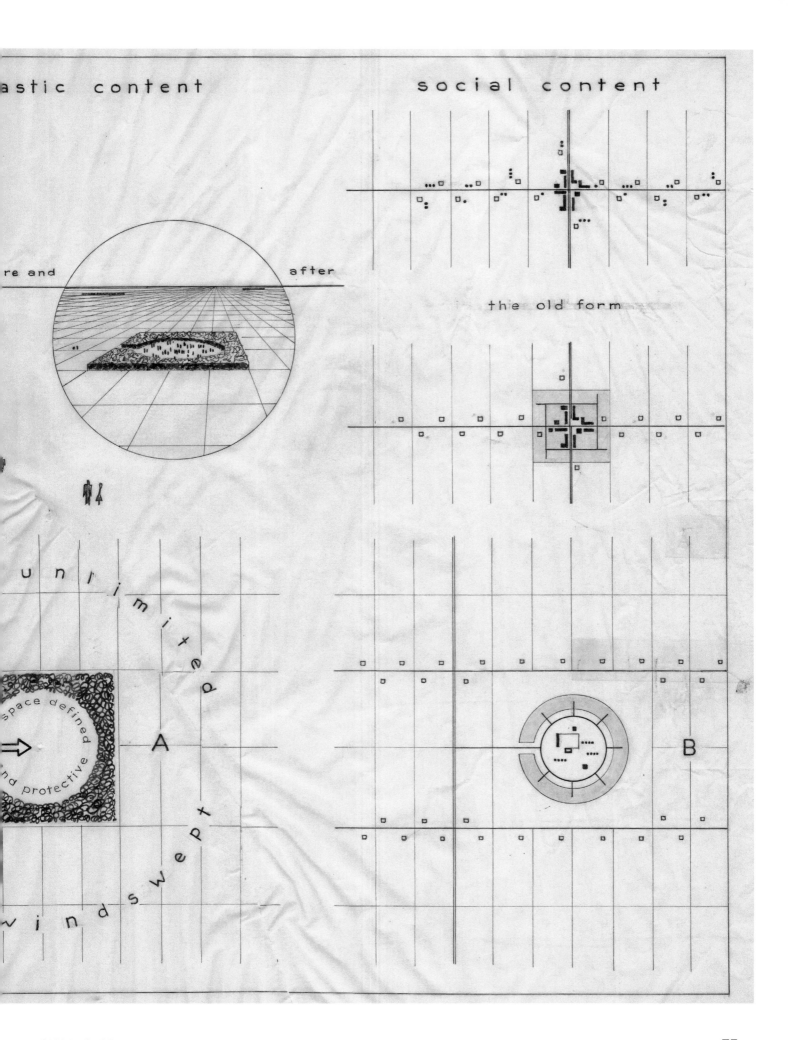

astic content

re and after

the old form

un l imited

A

space defined and protective

windswept

B

de 8 Amsterdam
Aldo van Eyck

Plan for Nagele, a village
in the Noordoostpolder

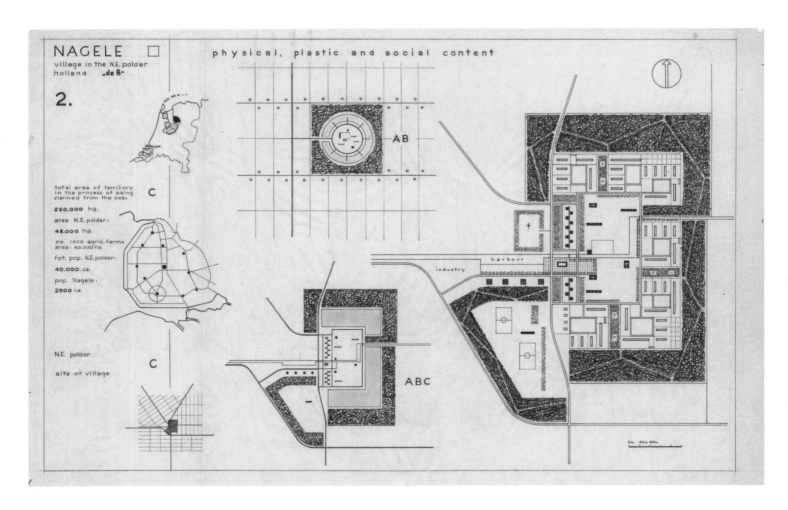

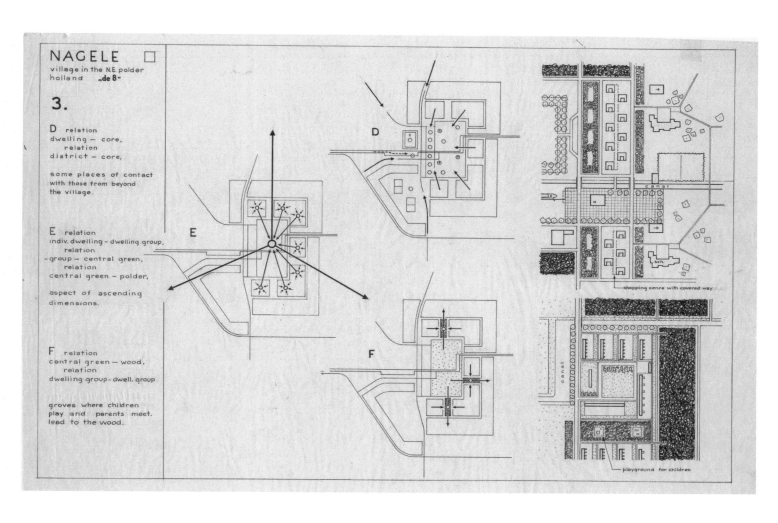

NAGELE ☐
village in the N.E. polder
holland „de 8"

3.

D relation
dwelling — core,
  relation
district — core,

some places of contact
with those from beyond
the village.

E relation
indiv. dwelling – dwelling group,
  relation
–group – central green,
  relation
central green – polder,

aspect of ascending
dimensions.

F relation
central green — wood,
  relation
dwelling group – dwell. group

groves where children
play and parents meet.
lead to the wood.

shopping centre with covered way

playground for children

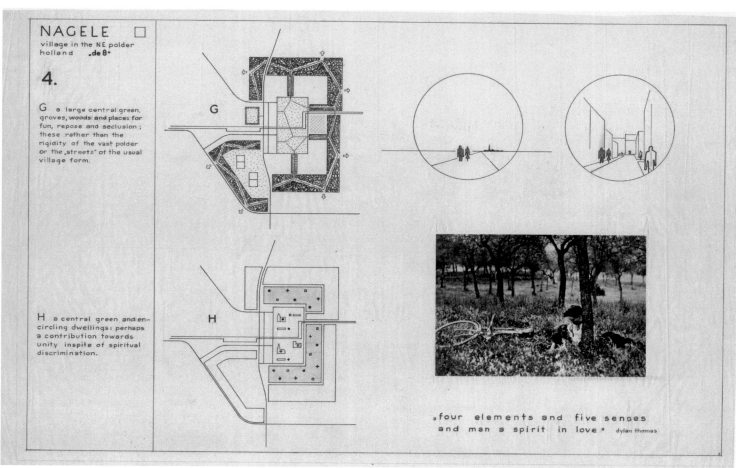

NAGELE ☐
village in the NE polder
holland „de 8"

4.

G a large central green,
groves, woods and places for
fun, repose and seclusion ;
these rather than the
rigidity of the vast polder
or the „streets" of the usual
village form.

H a central green and en-
circling dwellings: perhaps
a contribution towards
unity inspite of spiritual
discrimination.

„four elements and five senses
and man a spirit in love " dylan thomas

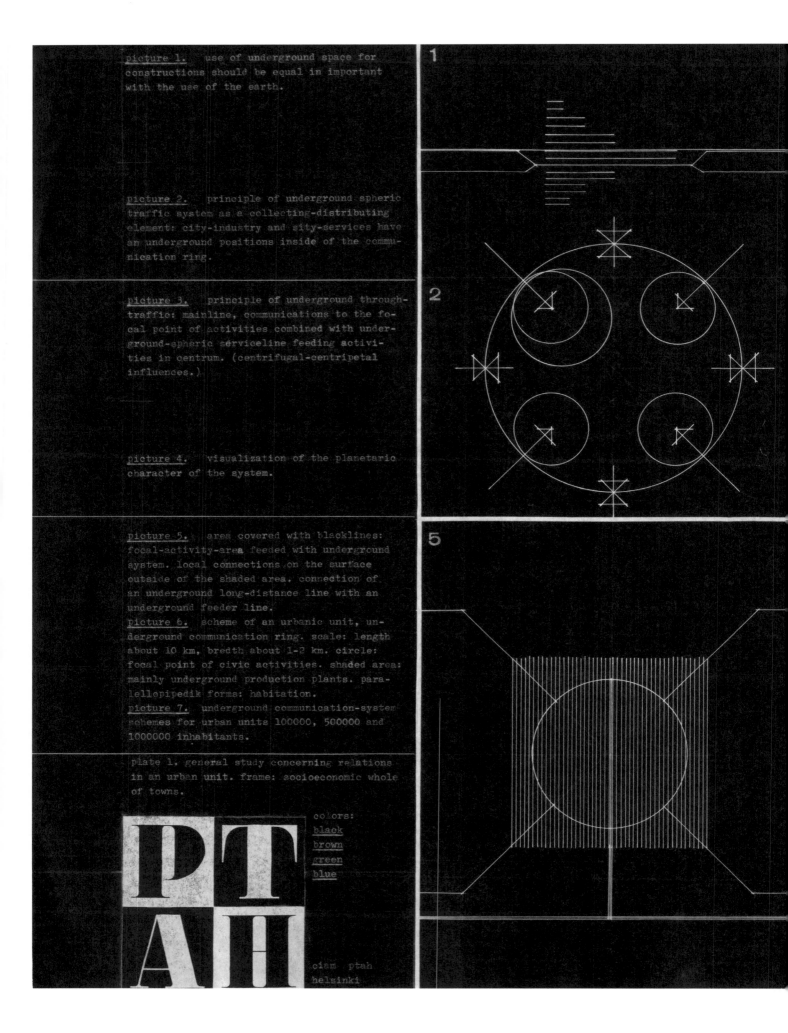

picture 1. use of underground space for constructions should be equal in important with the use of the earth.

picture 2. principle of underground spheric traffic system as a collecting-distributing element: city-industry and city-services have an underground positions inside of the communication ring.

picture 3. principle of underground through-traffic: mainline, communications to the focal point of activities combined with underground-spheric serviceline feeding activities in centrum. (centrifugal-centripetal influences.)

picture 4. visualization of the planetaric character of the system.

picture 5. area covered with blacklines: focal-activity-area feeded with underground system. local connections on the surface outside of the shaded area. connection of an underground long-distance line with an underground feeder line.

picture 6. scheme of an urbanic unit, underground communication ring. scale: length about 10 km, bredth about 1-2 km. circle: focal point of civic activities. shaded area: mainly underground production plants. paralellopipedik forms: habitation.

picture 7. underground communication-system schemes for urban units 100000, 500000 and 1000000 inhabitants.

plate 1. general study concerning relations in an urban unit. frame: socioeconomic whole of towns.

colors:
black
brown
green
blue

ciam ptah
helsinki

PTAH
Reima Pietilä

Proposal for an arctic
settlement

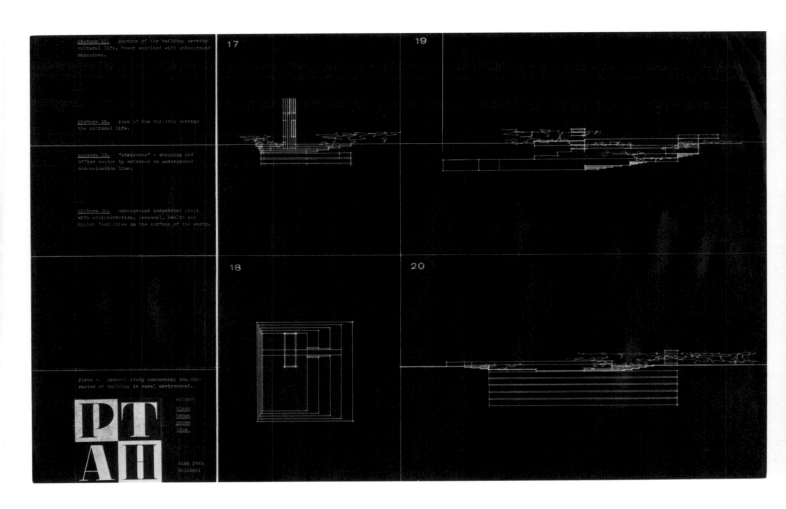

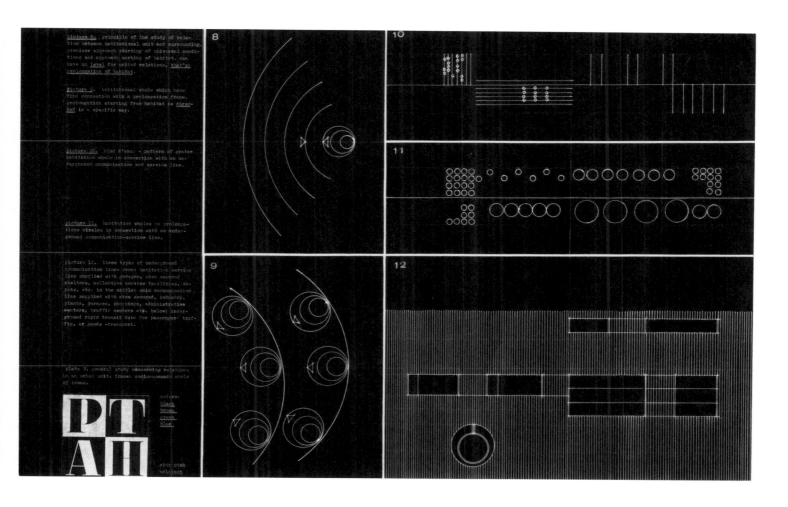

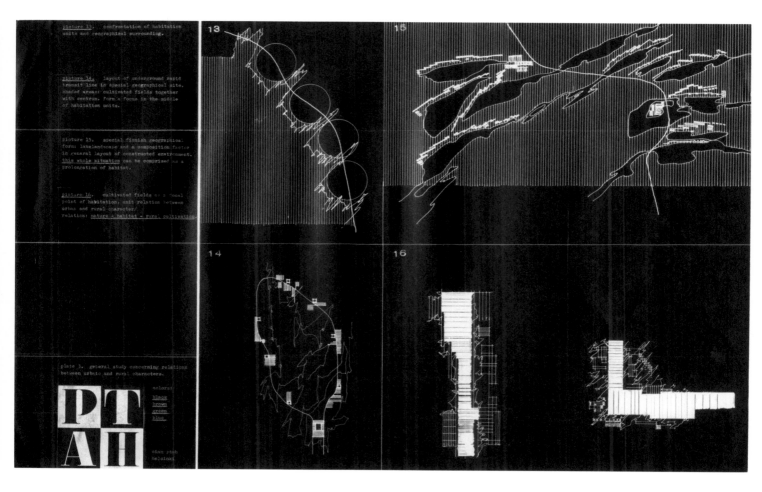

Georg Vrachliotis

FROM MICROCHIPS TO TOTAL CITIES

Fritz Haller's System Thinking

Fritz Haller and Konrad Wachsmann at the Institute for Building Research, University of Southern California in Los Angeles, 1966

1 Georg Vrachliotis, *Geregelte Verhältnisse: Architektur und technisches Denken in der Epoche der Kybernetik* (Vienna/New York: Springer, 2011).

2 Jürg Graser, *Gefüllte Leere: Das Bauen der Schule von Solothurn – Barth, Zaugg, Schlup, Füeg, Haller* (Zurich: gta Verlag, 2014); Laurent Stalder and Georg Vrachliotis (eds.), *Fritz Haller: Architekt und Forscher* (Zurich: gta Verlag, 2015).

3 Cf. Stiftung Bauhaus Dessau, The Art of Joining: Designing the Universal Connector, Bauhaus Taschenbuch No. 23 (Leipzig: Spector Books, 2018).

4 See: Hermann Herrey: 'At Last We Have a Prefabrication System Which Enables Architects to Design Any Type of Building with 3-Dimensional Modules: Konrad Wachsmann and Walter Gropius Produced the General Panel Corporation's Packaged Building', in: *New Pencil Points* 24 (April 1943), 36-47; Gilbert Herbert, *The Dream of the Factory-Made House* (Cambridge, MA/London: MIT Press, 1984).

5 The special issue on Konrad Wachsmann gives a good overview about his research, see: 'Konrad Wachsmann', *Bauen + Wohnen 10* (1960).

6 See: Monika Dommann, 'Systeme aus dem Mittelland', in: Stalder and Vrachliotis, *Fritz Haller*, op. cit. (note 2), 10-35.

7 For an overview of the history of the systems, see: 'Stahlbausysteme USM Haller Maxi, Mini, Midi 1961-1998, 1967, 1972-2000', in: Stalder and Vrachliotis, *Fritz Haller*, op. cit. (note 2), 253-263.

In the age of cybernetics, architects believed they were responsible for a future information society. Architects were caught up in the all-encompassing 'wave of demystification' unfolding 'under the auspices of the precise knowledge of information'. Concepts such as 'system' and 'structure' were given an explicitly technological sound and 'communication' no longer meant just a sense of community and collective identity, but also information technology, statistics and systems theory.[1]

The focus in architecture was therefore on the search for both aspects: the smallest spatial unit of coexistence, and a technological network model of social regulation based on communication and control. Such a network society implied a radical rethinking of the interconnectivity of scales. This was nothing less than an attempt by architecture to understand the philosophical concept of holism also in technological terms, and to make it the starting point for a new environment based on information and data.

One of the most remarkable and radical thinkers of a society understood in this way was Swiss architect Fritz Haller (1924-2012). Together with Alfons Barth, Franz Füeg, Max Schlup and Hans Zaugg, Haller was a member of the so-called Solothurn School.[2] His architectural thinking, like so many architects of his generation, was shaped by his personal experience of the post-war period.

The Universal Connector

Haller was to be heavily influenced by another great system thinker in twentieth-century modern architecture, German architect Konrad Wachsmann (1901-1980), and in many ways, Haller would further develop Wachsmann's project. Haller got to know Wachsmann when the latter was leading a workshop on system design at the École Polytechnique de l'Université de Lausanne (now EPFL) in 1959. Haller was one of the participants. With his research work, Wachsmann delved deep into the mechanical logic of mass production and the automation industry. As early as the mid-1940s, Wachsmann had developed one of the world's first fully automatic construction industry facilities. For him, the research focus was therefore not on the individual building, but on the system; not on the object, but on the series; not on the craft, but on the automation. It involved experimental thinking in variants and prototypes. The main focus of Wachsmann's research was concerned with the art of joining industrialized, prefabricated elements by way of a standardized, connecting element, and crucially and ideally three-dimensionally.[3] The search for a such a universal

connector combined his interest in the rationalization and standardization concepts of universal applicability. The universal connector was a metal connecting node utilized in the construction of prefabricated houses. A first application was successfully realized in 1949, with the General Panel System designed by Wachsmann together with Walter Gropius.[4]

Wachsmann organized a series of international workshops in those years to promote his research, such as the aforementioned workshop in Lausanne, but for example also with Egon Eiermann in Karlsruhe (1954), with Kenzo Tange in Tokyo (1955), and famously for the Salzburg Summer Academy (1956-1959).[5] Besides his research on the universal connector, Wachsmann gradually introduced a second focus: the question of how to work best together as a group. Like in a factory, work processes in the building industry were increasingly broken down into individual steps, and thus, crucially, the systematization of building went hand in hand with the systematization of knowledge and its application.

Haller was fascinated by these two forms of systematization – of building systems and of knowledge, and for good reason: at the time, he was developing prefabricated school buildings for the local government in Switzerland, such as the Cantonal School Baden (1962-1964) and the Brugg-Windisch Institute of Advanced Technical Training (1964-1966). Working along the same lines as Wachsmann before him – but not yet as sophisticated – Haller was interested in how systems could be used not only to shape architectural space, but also to structure knowledge production and learning processes.

Modular Systems

In the early 1960s, the company USM commissioned Haller to design a flexible manufacturing facility in Münsingen, a small village near the Swiss capital Bern.[6] To this end, in 1963 Haller developed the 'USM Haller MAXI', a modular steel construction system. The supporting structure was based on a basic module measuring 14.40 x 14.40 m, which could be extended horizontally – a quality especially important for industrial buildings. Haller followed this with two more modular building systems: 'USM Haller MINI', a system suited for two-storey private homes measuring 8.40 m wide; and the 'USM Haller MIDI', for multi-storey structures with integrated installations, up to 16.8 m wide.[7] All three steel construction systems were based on a module measuring 1.20 x 1.20 m. This was a common dimension in the Swiss building industry for the manufacture of so-called semi-finished panel structures. Instead of inventing a completely new order,

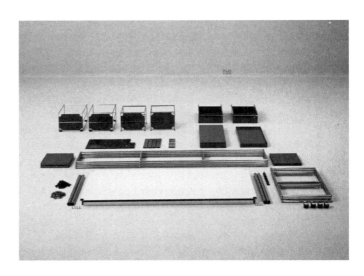

Fritz Haller, Cantonal School, Baden, 1962-1964

USM Haller factory in Münsingen, southeast view, c. 1966

Disassembled USM Haller furniture system, c. 1967

View into USM's office building, furnished with the first version of USM Haller furniture system, shortly after completion, 1965

8   See: Niklaus Emanuel Deutsch (ed.), Zeitprobleme in der Schweizer Malerei und Plastik, exhibition catalogue (Zurich: Kunsthaus Zurich, 1936); Hans Frei, Konkrete Architektur? Über Max Bill als Architekt (Baden: Lars Müller, 1991).

9   Richard Paul Lohse, 'Normung als Strukturprinzip', Werk 61/3 (1974), 347-353.

10   Fritz Haller, 'von eigenschaften ausgezeichneter punkte in regulären geometrischen systemen', manuscript (July 1967), 9; gta Archiv, ETH Zurich: Fritz Haller Archive, No. 189-12-5.

11   See: Annemarie Jaeggi (ed.), Egon Eiermann (1904-1970): Die Kontinuität der Moderne (Ostfildern-Ruit: Hatje Cantz Verlag, 2004).

12   In 1956, Steinbuch coined the word Informatik (Informatics) in a paper he published under the title 'Informatik: Automatische Informationsverarbeitung' in SEG-Nachrichten (Technische Mitteilungen der Standard Elektrik Gruppe), Berlin, 1957. See also: Die informierte Gesellschaft: Geschichte und Zukunft der Nachrichtentechnik (Stuttgart: Deutsche Verlagsanstalt, 1966).

for him it was about finding rational forms to further develop something that already existed. It was about improving the connectivity of architecture to existing production norms in the building industry, about the architectural and aesthetic refinement of the system idea itself, and about a conceptual radicalization of the very notion of standardization.

One of Haller's most famous systems is the 'USM Haller furniture system', which went into production in 1963. Like a three-dimensional stacking game, its components can be infinitely reorganized and expanded. Regardless of whether it was a building or a furniture system, montage – understood as the sequential coordination and control of the assembly of building components – served as a key mechanism, both structurally and theoretically, in all of Haller's system environments. But in contrast to his furniture system, Haller's building systems were 'open systems', meaning that components from other systems could also be integrated into the supporting structure. This structural openness was one of the most important qualities of Haller's building systems.

The elegance of many of Fritz Haller's projects recalls the geometric aesthetics of Concrete Art as theorized by among others Max Bill.[8] However, he was not interested in establishing an analogy between standardized architecture and painting, unlike Swiss painter Richard Paul Lohse, for instance, who established a connection between Wachsmann's building systems and his own paintings in his essay 'Standardization as a Structural Principal' (1974).[9] Instead, Haller wanted to create a super-classification for construction systems, an abstract meta-system for architecture. Every system, Haller argued, had 'characteristic properties in terms of its geometry, the manner of its assembly, and the flow of forces. It must be possible to organize systems on the basis of these three characteristics.'[10] Essentially, Haller was interested in something that one could call the structural performance of systems.

Architecture Systems and Computer Systems

Between 1966 and 1971, Haller would serve as a visiting researcher at Wachsmann's Institute of Building Research at the University of Southern California in Los Angeles. After that Haller was considered for a professorship at the University of Stuttgart, but due to institutional opposition he did not get the job. Evidently, the serial thinking of prefabrication was no longer a priority for the university, which also happened to be home to Frei Otto's Institute for Lightweight Structures, founded in 1964. Otto's notion of 'organic architecture' had become internationally *en vogue*, thanks to the

pavilion for Expo 67 in Montreal (with Rudolf Gutbrod), the Olympic site for Munich 72 (with Günter Behnisch), and the Multihalle 1975 (with Carlfried Mutschler). Otto's tent roofs and gridshells – which were embedded in the topography of the landscape, and almost appeared to float – were a built antithesis to Haller's grids and building systems. Otto's structures showed a way beyond standardization in architecture.

Ultimately, Haller accepted an appointment as professor at the Technical University of Karlsruhe. In fact, this post at the more traditional school in Karlsruhe made perfect sense. Haller was well integrated into the thought collective (*Denkkollektiv*) on prefabricated construction that Egon Eiermann had established there, during his tenure from 1948 to 1970. Eiermann was regarded as one of the most influential architects and teachers of the German post-war period. With his elegant pavilions of glass and steel and delicate industrial and corporate buildings, he shaped architectural thinking in Germany for decades.[11] Haller, who by then had made a name for himself, especially through the facility for USM in Münsingen, was a good match for the scene in Karlsruhe. Crucially, apart from the architectural tradition, there was another interesting aspect as well: electrical engineer Karl Steinbuch, a pioneer and specialist for 'self-correcting circuits', had helped Karlsruhe become an internationally influential centre for cybernetics and early computer science.[12] The overlapping of these two traditional lines of system thinking – of standardized construction and computer research – resulted in a fruitful intellectual and technological milieu that Haller used to his advantage. Even before the computer would firmly establish itself within architectural practice, Haller's focus there was on the experimental and speculative examination of the notion of environment in the digital age.

The City as a Technological Web

Haller's time with Wachsmann in Los Angeles, and his personal experience of the sprawled city, strongly influenced his further intellectual development. Haller transposed the vastness and hugeness of the Californian metropolis onto his native Swiss context, and transformed the transport networks of LA into strict traffic charts on graph paper. He took the previously understood notion of 'system' in architecture and radicalized and expanded upon it at various scales. In other words: the city becomes a technological network of interconnected scales and infrastructure becomes a medium of integration.

This radicalization was strongly reflected in two urban studies Haller produced on the so-called 'Totale Stadt' or 'Total City'. The first, published in 1968 was

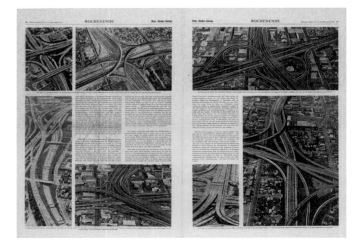

**Frei Otto, with Rudolf Gutbrod,
Expo Pavilion in Montreal, 1967**

**'Die Stadt, die eigentlich keine
ist: Los Angeles im Fluge', article
published in the *Neue Zürcher
Zeitung*, 24 January 1971**

**View into the interior of an
electronic unit of an IBM
computer**

13   Cf. Laurent Stalder, 'Raster,
Netzwerk, Register: Fritz Hallers
Totale Stadt', in: Stalder and
Vrachliotis, *Fritz Haller*, op. cit.
(note 2), 92-107.
14   Pierre Teilhard de Chardin,
'The Phases and Future of the
Noosphere', in: Pierre Teilhard de
Chardin, *The Future of Man* (New
York: Harper and Row, 1969).
15   Teilhard de Chardin as quoted
by Fritz Haller in: 'Erinnerung an
die Zeit in 150 Jahren', Rede an der
Veranstaltung 150 Jahre SIA,
Kopf und Maschine aus der Sicht
von Wissenschaft, Philosophie
und Architektur, 24.10.1987
(gta:1970-2002 07 189–3), 8-9.
Originally published in: Pierre

Teilhard de Chardin, *Aufstieg zur
Einheit: Die Zukunft der menschlichen
Evolution*, edited by Lorenz Häfliger
(Vienna: Buchgemeinschaft
Donauland, 1974), translation by
the author.
16   Cf. Pierre Teilhard de Chardin,
Der Mensch im Kosmos (Munich:
C.H. Beck, 1959); David Pitt and
Paul R. Samson (eds.), *The Biosphere
and Noosphere Reader: Global
Environment, Society and Change*
(Oxon: Routledge, 1998).
17   Marshall McLuhan, *The
Gutenberg Galaxy* (Toronto:
University of Toronto Press, 1962),
32.

titled 'Totale Stadt – ein Modell' ('Total City – a Model'); the second followed in 1975, titled 'Totale Stadt – ein globales Modell' ('Total City – a Global Model'). In large-scale diagrams of impressive elegance, drawn by hand by his wife Therese Beyeler, Haller envisioned a futuristic society that was wholly regulated by infrastructure.

The main part of Haller's first investigation was dedicated to the building of urban systems. These ranged from the smallest unit, the so-called 'unit of zero order', which consisted of a place to sleep, to rest and watch TV, and a family dining space, to the 'unit of the fourth order', which included 61 million people. The system he developed was an intricate, interlaced urban system with a conceptual framework based on the search for a technically and geometrically optimized infrastructure. Similar to a giant computer network, Haller worked with individual nodes in a decentralized communication system that, due to its high degree of abstraction, could be imagined on a global scale as well as on the scale of a city or landscape. The individual character of a space was not paramount in this system, but rather the potential for integration in a smoothly organized functional matrix. The extreme systematization of space shown here turned out to be an arrangement on different scales: structural nodes became transport nodes, which eventually became communication nodes.

The 'Totale Stadt' project constituted a system of resting and moving objects and energies.[13] What held the plan together was not a spatial arrangement, but an infrastructural one, defined primarily by transportation routes interlinking the various points or traffic nodes in the grid.

Haller's basic premise was that individual nodes in a decentralized communication system could be considered not only on an urban scale, but also on a global scale. Along similar lines, Arata Isozaki's 'Computer-Aided City' project (1972) is a clear demonstration of how strongly architects believed at the time that the social space could be precisely regulated and controlled by technical models. More radically speaking, the issue was to systematize the so-called socializing function of space.

In contrast to Haller's universal furniture systems, however, his 'Totale Stadt' projects provoked an enormous amount of criticism. The systematization of living space (*Lebensraum*) that Haller's drawings represented called to mind, especially in West Germany, the all-too-recent notion of a totalitarian state.

Yet, Haller was by no means the only person thinking along these lines. Many architects at the time were looking at the conceptualization of process characteristics – such as adaptability, organization and regulation – as a way of responding to the widespread

perception of a changing and increasingly technical world. But instead of dealing with similar examples from architecture, Haller cited French philosopher and theologian Pierre Teilhard de Chardin – a reference that bordered on the esoteric. It was because of him that Haller dared to call his city model 'total'. Teilhard saw the technical world as a 'huge totalization machine' on the path to 'social totalization'.[14] It is therefore not surprising that Haller quoted Teilhard's *Ascent to Unity* (1974) in retrospect to explain his two city models:

> We don't understand how the amazing system – of land, sea, and air routes, of postal links, wires and cables, which span the face of the earth more and more with each passing day – forms before our eyes. 'It's all just for business or entertaining communications,' we are repeatedly told; 'the production of utility pathways and commercial channels…' Not at all, we say; it's much more profound than that, it's the creation of a nervous system of humanity; the development of a common consciousness, the cementing of the human masses. …While we are developing the roads, the railways, the airplane, the press and the radio, we believe we are merely talking, just doing our business or just spreading ideas… In reality, for a view that combines the general plan of human movement and that of the movements of every physical organism, we are simply continuing the uninterrupted work of biological evolution at a higher level and by other means.[15]

Teilhard envisioned the emergence of what he called a 'noosphere'.[16] With this, he meant a kind of layer of collective human consciousness that surrounds the entire earth and connects all people with one another – just as the brain connects myriads of nerve cells and enables creative thinking. It's not surprising that none other than Marshall McLuhan repeatedly referred to Teilhard. McLuhan wrote:

> This externalization of our senses creates what de Chardin calls the 'noosphere' or a technological brain for the world. Instead of tending towards a vast Alexandrian library the world has become a computer, an electronic brain, exactly as in an infantile piece of science fiction.[17]

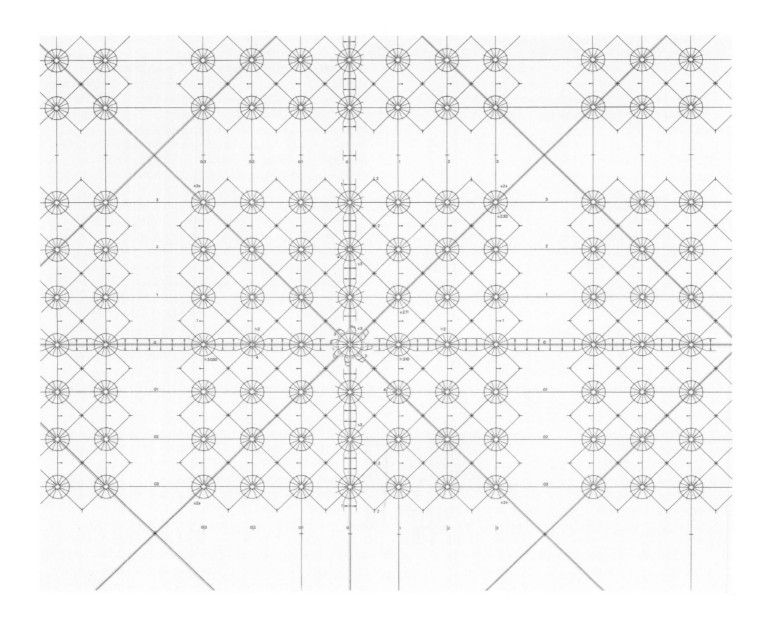

Fritz Haller, Totale Stadt. Ein Globales Modell. Zweite Studie (Integral Urban. A Global Model. Second Study), 1975. Drawings by Therese Beyeler

18   Fritz Haller: 'Allgemeinen Lösung', 19 January 1978, transcript; gta Archiv, ETH Zurich: Fritz Haller Archive, No. 189-T-1-4, no page numbers.
19   Jürg Graser, *Die Schule von Solothurn: Der Beitrag von Alfons Barth, Hans Zaugg, Max Schlup, Franz Füeg und Fritz Haller zur Schweizer Architektur der zweiten Hälfte des 20. Jahrhunderts*, PhD dissertation (ETH Zurich, 2008), appendix, II.
20   Martin Burckhardt, *Metamorphosen von Raum und Zeit: Eine Geschichte der Wahrnehmung* (Frankfurt am Main/New York: Campus, 1994), 312.

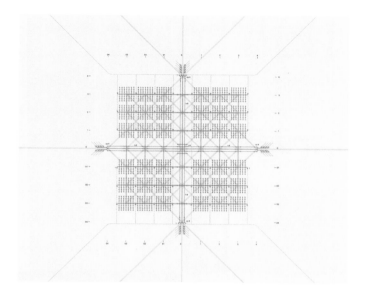

Microchips

While much in the age of cybernetics had revolved around operationality, methods and processes – and not around concrete, material, objective realities – a new, abstract, technology-based visual imagery emerged in the work of Haller. Following the enthusiasm for rationalization and scientification, and the increasing miniaturization of technology in the 1970s and 1980s, his attention shifted to the structure and design of microchips. There was the discovery of hardware itself. The microchip directed the gaze to the computer's physical dimension. And so it was no coincidence that Haller spoke immediately about the structure of microchips in his first lecture in Karlsruhe in 1974. As with the assembly processes in standardized, industrial construction, the millions of transistors, capacitors and resistors must be connected in the correct sequence in time and space in order to fit on the silicon wafer, which is only a few square millimetres in size. According to Haller, microchips are therefore 'phenomena that are very similar to what we know from the history of building'.[18] In an interview at the end of the 1990s Haller took this idea even further, declaring:

> If you see the chip as an image in a greatly enlarged scale, it resembles Mondrian's images. This is the new world. The structure of a chip is like the structure of a house. The chips can't be fathomed by our senses. This frightens us, and we think that it's inhuman. But this is where the world really begins...[19]

The microchip symbolized a perfect description of frictionless architecture as a technical structure. One way to describe a microchip is that it is nothing more than an 'extreme agglomeration of that network space as it was in the nineteenth century', as philosopher Martin Burkhardt commented in 1997.[20] The complex overlapping of the filigree grids of vertical and horizontal circuits, and the geometrically balanced arrangement of the wires lead to a playful confrontation with the fiction of the technical in the eye of the beholder. In the scalelessness of the circuits, the microchip transforms into an intricate pattern of cables, wires, buildings or even an entire city. Under the influence of a world characterized by increasing miniaturization and virtualization processes, Haller no longer saw transformable building systems as a starting point, but the world as a database. In this he differed from Wachsmann, who was mainly interested in the automation of construction, not in the development of corresponding tools. Haller's originality as a researcher consisted in his transformation of system thinking on industrial building into the operative and scalelessness of the visual logic of information technology.

Hadas A. Steiner

A HABITAT WAITING TO BE

The Northern Aviary in the London Zoo

**Cedric Price with Frank Newby,
London Zoo Aviary, Regent's
Park, London, 1961-1965**

**Berthold Lubetkin, Penguin Pool
at the London Zoo, 1934**

1   The reasons behind this are outlined by Paul Lawrence Farber in *Discovering Birds: The Emergence of Ornithology as a Scientific Discipline, 1760-1850* (Baltimore: Johns Hopkins University Press, 1997).

2   See, for example, Darwin's *Ornithological Notes*, edited by Nora Barlow (London: Bulletin of the British Museum Historical Series, 1963).

3   Henry Eliot Howard, *The British Warblers: A History with Problems of Their Lives* (London: R.H. Porter, 1907-1914); Henry Eliot Howard, *An Introduction to the Study of Bird Behavior* (Cambridge: Cambridge University Press, 1929); and Henry Eliot Howard, *Territory in Bird Life* (London: John Murray, 1920).

4   François Jacob, *The Logic of Life* (Princeton: Princeton University Press, 1993), 111.

5   This story has been told, for example, by Peder Anker in *From Bauhaus to Ecohouse: A History of Ecological Design* (Baton Rouge, LA: LSU Press, 2010).

6   In conversation with the author. His private library held two annotated copies of the book, as catalogued in: Eleanor Bron and Samantha Hardingham (eds.), *Cedric Price Retriever* (London: Iniva, 2006), 49.

7   See Martha Adams Bohrer, 'Tales of Locale: *The Natural History of Selborne* and *Castle Rackrent*', *Modern Philology* 100/3 (2003), 319-416: 403.

8   The Linnaean Society of London was itself founded in 1788.

9   Sir Stamford Raffles, the colonial founder of Singapore, returned from the Far East with a starter crop of specimens. As Raffles conceived them, the collections of the London Zoological Gardens were intended scientifically to trump those at the first such institution, the Jardin des Plantes in Paris.

Milieu

Though a birdcage seems an unlikely manifestation of the architectural conception of habitat, the Northern Aviary in the London Zoo (1961), designed by architect Cedric Price with structural engineer Frank Newby, is just that – right from the subjects viewed through its crystalline frame. Indeed, birds, or more accurately the study of birds, had guided the development of ecological theory by leading the paradigmatic shift from morphological investigations of dead laboratory specimens to surveying the activity of living creatures.[1] Avian behaviour further guided developments fundamental to the discipline of natural history at large. Darwin, for a renowned example, claimed that the observations of live birds inspired his evolutionary speculations.[2] Later, Henry Eliot Howard would define the paradigm of territory through the analysis of the courtship habits of warblers.[3] The conduct of geese led Konrad Lorenz and Nikolaas Tinbergen to establish the field of ethology. Such behavioural insights, all vital to the conception of habitat, would be overtly extended to the human sphere in influential texts written as the Northern Aviary took shape, most prominently *The Territorial Imperative* (1966) by Robert Ardrey and *The Hidden Dimension* (1966) by Edward T. Hall.

The research of living organisms rendered modern biology a spatial project that investigated

> …the way in which living beings were arranged in space: not only the space in which all beings were disposed, broken into separate islands and carved into independent series – but also the space in which the organism itself took up its abode, coiled round a nucleus, formed by successive layers that extended beyond the living being, linking it to its surroundings.[4]

The development of ecological science early in the twentieth century was a direct outcome of this conceptualization of biology as inherently spatial. Developments in biology were intertwined with the repercussions of the habitat model for architecture that began to be debated among scientists with a social agenda. Such discussions were predominantly focused on the subject of housing as a social, health and formal problem. If the individual house was correctly configured, architecture as a whole would provide an ecosystem that cultivated the well-being of a society.

Several British ornithologists who were particularly active in the establishment of ecological science also engaged in political activism geared towards an overhaul of working-class accommodations. Tom Harrisson, for example, one of the founders of the social research organization Mass Observation,

diverted his ornithological gaze to the study of humans and argued the case for housing reform. Julian Huxley, whose career began with definitive research on grebes, became an advocate for the popularization of ecological science, as well as for human welfare. Huxley would use his influence, and later his position as Secretary of the Zoological Society (1935-1942), to foster a dialogue between the biologists in his circle and the modernist architects in exile from Germany regarding the design for animal and human habitats.[5] As a result, the pavilions for primates and penguins at the London Zoo were among the first modernist structures to be built in Britain. Huxley's legacy continued in other commissions, including a Brutalist enclosure for elephants and, of course, a tensegrity structure for birds.

Terrain

The design for an aviary in this context suited the idiosyncratic interests of Cedric Price. Price admired *The Natural History and Antiquities of Selborne* (1789), the classic proto-ecological text by clergyman Gilbert White.[6] On the face of it, the *Natural History* was a meticulous environmental survey of an isolated parish in the south of England. White, however, drew insight primarily from the scrutiny of animal behaviour. He was also aware that the new binomial taxonomy introduced by Linnaeus could not account for his own identifications of species via their patterns, such as those of procreation, comportment and communication – elements now classed as ethological. Local observations made White evermore aware of the effects of distant events on his milieu and of the global circulation of species. White took a keen interest in verifying the cycle of bird migration, for example, which at the time was not fully understood, or even accepted. Selborne was the vehicle by which the seventeenth-century concept of habitat as a favoured location of a particular species was broadened to embrace an ecosystem of interdependent animal classes.[7] Under the guise of the very local lay the call for an interpretation of nature as a dynamically related series of components in which a whole would always be more than the sum of its parts.

By the time the Zoological Club of the Linnaean Society came into being in 1822, White's focus on animal behaviour, territory and breeding habits had taken root among its members.[8] That group then formed the Zoological Society of London in 1826 as a venue for such study.[9] That zoo and its gardens famously set the bar for the many urban zoos to follow in two major regards: for the use of taxonomic principles to order scientific investigation and for the setting of the collection within a 'naturalistic' landscape

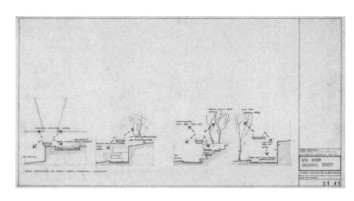

View of the cliff, with Lord
Snowdon, Cedric Price
and Frank Newby, c. 1965

Diagram showing a view
of bird activities in relation
to architecture

Promotional brochure
produced by the London Zoo
for the opening of the
Snowdon Aviary, 1965

10   Hadas A. Steiner, 'For the
Birds', *Grey Room* 13 (2004), 5-31.
11   Snowdon was best known for
capturing the spirit of London
in the 1960s through intimate
portraits of artists, writers, actors
and designers. His brother-in-law,
the Duke of Edinburgh and the
president of the Zoological Society,
recommended him for the job.
12   Price had collaborated with
Fuller in the late 1950s on a design
for an auditorium that would extend
the geodesic radome system to
the programme of concerts.
The design, known as the Claverton
Dome, was never built. Newby
would also consult with Fuller on
details regarding the anchoring
of the tie-down plates.

13   Minutes for the Working Party
on Future Policy on Bird Collections,
6 April 1961, 2.
14   Jon Charles Coe, 'Towards a
Co-Evolution of Zoos, Aquariums
and Natural History Museums',
*AAZPA 1986 Annual Conference
Proceedings*, American Association
of Zoological Parks and Aquariums,
Wheeling, WV, 366-376.
15   Minutes for the Working Party
on Future Policy on Bird Collections,
6 April 1961, 2.
16   Letter from the Controller
Major-General CJG Dalton to Price,
5 November 1962.

of a public park.[10] Design strategy and scientific technique, both, were deployed to bring a landscape of the kind that White had found at his doorstep into the by now fully industrialized conditions of modern England. When Huxley led the call for modernist accommodations in the 1930s, territorial mimicry was the design trend in zoological habitats. The abstract modernist alternative rejected the illusion of habitat in favour of one determined by use. But by 1953, when institutional modernism as represented by the CIAM was itself proposing to replace the functionalist Charter of Athens with one of Habitat, the zoo was confronting the insufficiencies of its visitor circulation and animal facilities, as well as structural damage that had occurred during the Blitz. The charismatic Lord Zuckerman was brought in as Secretary in 1955 to address these problems and he hired Sir Hugh Casson, the knighted architectural director of the Festival of Britain, to spearhead a site plan for a 'New Zoo.'

Anticipating the physical changes afoot, the Collections Policy Committee produced memoranda, such as the one dedicated to the 'Future Policy on Bird Collections', to advocate for its needs and influence the design process. In November of 1960, in keeping with Zuckerman's penchant for social connections and modern design, the Zoological Society of London invited celebrity photographer Antony Armstrong-Jones, known as the Earl of Snowdon after his marriage to Princess Margaret, to design a new walk-through aviary to replace the Great Aviary of 1888.[11] It was Snowdon who brought Cedric Price, a licensed friend from his university days, in as an associate. Price then solicited the collaboration of Frank Newby, who had recently taken over the firm of his mentor, Felix Samuely, whose approach to structures as dynamic entities had been inspirational to Price during his diploma years at the Architectural Association School of Architecture in London.

Territory

Starting from a series of preliminary sketches prepared by Price, Newby proposed a tension structure with distinctive peaks using the concept of tensegrity learned from Buckminster Fuller.[12] The inhabitants, it was determined, would be drawn from a 'habitat group comprising tropical and subtropical birds appropriate to an environment broadly representative of Africa and India'.[13] No other species were to be included. In the zoological setting, solely birds from a large swath bound together only in that they evolved in a similar climate range, and would not ordinarily establish territory in such proximity, would have to dwell among vegetation that could thrive in London under unusually acidic conditions.

The Zoological Society brass responded positively to the preliminary proposal. Criticism of the cage, however, reflected the views held by most Society members for what constituted appropriate exhibit design – essentially an animate version of museum dioramas that combined taxidermy with artificial props and elaborately painted backgrounds.[14] Territory in this live case required the accommodation of water birds, ground-dwelling birds, cliff-nesting birds, and tree and bush-nesting birds: four categories of breeding behaviour in a single spatial vignette. The committee repeatedly stated that it was 'strongly in favour of providing a naturalistic background for the birds', but given the artificial demographic there was no version of a non-captive habitat to capture. Rather, they requested features that would symbolize the natural world to the observer.

Mimicry, on the other hand, did not interest Price.

Habitat

The feature that most rankled was the centrepiece: a concrete cliff-face that was to provide nesting, perching and feeding facilities to enable birds that had never before reared young in captivity to reproduce. 'It was emphasized', the zoo insisted again and again as the two sides tussled over the textural treatment of the concrete surface, 'that the greatest care must be taken to produce rockwork which would look convincing even to a geologist'.[15] It was suggested that mouldings be made from 'natural cliff and rock'. Meanwhile, Price continued to insist on a shuttered grain. Price's strategy bypassed the processes of pictorial analogy, along with the assumption that subjective experience of wildlife encounters should be projected by placing the emphasis squarely on the process of abstraction. The zoo, in turn, protested against what they called 'this very formalized treatment of the cliff'.[16] Casson, in his role as master planner, acted as adjudicator between Price and the increasingly exasperated Controller, and negotiated a truce whereby the spirit of the proposal was mediated through a framework in which all the parts of the concrete work would be treated in the same abstract manner despite the different natural features it assembled. Construct was thus made tolerable to the realist through a modernist gloss of compositional unity.

The palpable presence of the aluminium members that constituted the cage, especially in comparison with their equivalent in steel, was another feature that worked against expert opinion. *Avicultural Magazine* reported that the structure interfered with the illusion of walking among free birds.[17] Architects meanwhile complained that the structural members were too

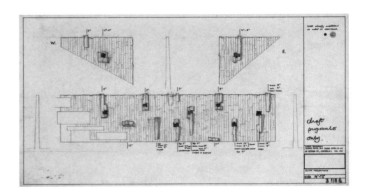

Entrance to the aviary

Elevation of the cliff, 1963

17 'There has recently been a frightening outburst of bad taste in zoo designing; fantastically shaped and coloured houses, cages, and aviaries are being planned. I was saddened recently at seeing the ugly and inadequate gibbon cage now being built at the London Zoo (on whose Council I served for many years) and still more so by the project of an aviary – a fussy, ridiculously shaped, 'horned' horror which is not only in bad taste, but impracticable and unsuitable. The principle of a 'walk-in' cage is excellent ... But its very principle is that the cage itself is not obvious, so that the visitor who is inside has as much as possible the illusion of walking among free birds. The frame of the aviary must not only be simple and inconspicuous, but also made invisible by trees and creepers. Even its approach should be so planted on the outside that one is not aware that there is a cage at all ... We show natural objects which have themselves a great attraction – they do not require outside help to call the visitors attention.' Jean Delacour, 'Cage and Aviary Design,' *The Avicultural Magazine*, May-June 1961.

18 Reyner Banham, 'Aviary, London Zoological Gardens', in: *A Critic Writes: Essays by Reyner Banham* (Los Angeles: University of California Press, 1996), 119-121. First published in *Architectural Review* 138 (September 1965), 186.

19 'Bird's Nest Robberies Leave Zoo with Egg on its Face', *Tri City Herald*, 28 November 1972.

20 Minutes of the Working Party on Future Policy for Bird Collections, 16 December 1964, London Zoological Society Archives, London.

21 Buckminster Fuller to Frank Newby, Box DR 1995 0185:275 (3/4), Cedric Price Archive, Canadian Centre for Architecture, Montreal.

22 Will Alsop, 'Flights of Fancy', *The Guardian*, 18 June 2005.

23 *Architectural Design* **35** (September 1965), 454.

24 'Engineers and Architects: Newby+Price', *AA Files* 27 (summer 1994), 30.

chunky to be pleasing.[18] Moreover, the manufacture of aluminium parts at this scale was laborious and meant that five different companies had to be contracted. Yet the case for aluminium was found to be justifiable by the Society. Among the significant environmental conditions caused by birds penned in captivity, is the accumulation of acidic feces that corrode material finishes, harbour disease and kill plantings that provide facilities for the birds. The structure of the aviary was a key element in resolving how a closed environment could evolve as it would outside.

To complement the non-corrosive material, a special pump was installed to provide the waterpower required to clean the pinnacles of the structure. Various techniques, including air blast devices used near runways, were also investigated by the zoo to keep the birds away from these hard-to-clean areas. Maintenance was on equal footing with other deliberations of the design process, and Price repeatedly deflected the demands for an unobtrusive entrance for service personnel.

The give and take between architect and zoo continually focused on the points where the design confronted the interaction of organisms, from rockwork to cage to plants: between birds of different species, birds and their curators, the plants and their landscape, the structure and the maintenance crew, birds and their visitors, and aviary and zoo. These intersections and the controls installed at them were recurrently pressured by variable circumstances: the configuration of human entry and exit, which was exhaustively calculated to enable pedestrian flow while keeping the birds in, for example, did not exclude vandals who stripped nests of rare eggs.[19]

The gaps in the latticework were calculated to be small enough to keep aggressive city birds such as starlings out of the habitat at the same time as they had to be large enough to resist icing. Too late in the process to adapt the weave because a smaller gap would have increased the loading by 50 per cent, the working module (6 x 1 1/8', or 15.2 x 2.8 cm) proved to admit foraging sparrows. A patrol of hawks was proposed to counter that infiltration – in this case to guard against birds coming in rather than getting out.[20] Buckminster Fuller wrote to Newby expressing his concern that resident birds would get caught in and break the mesh in the struggle to get free. 'To build the vast tetrahedral,' he added, 'emphasizing triangular stability, and to wire it with a linking of quadrangular, easily breakable veil is not aesthetically sound, let alone politically safe.'[21] Price, for his part, preferred to treat captivity as a temporary condition. He claimed 'that once the community was established, it would be possible to remove the netting. The skin was a temporary feature: it only needed to be there long enough for the birds to feel at home.'[22] In short, it was only needed to achieve the dynamic condition of homeostasis, or the active state of equilibrium.

Environment

The experimental form of this tension structure began with an investigation of the possible configurations of cable networks carried by a supporting framework. Because of their special interest in tensegrity, Price and Newby focused on the options where suspended compression members also acted as vertical cantilevers. The pair was particularly interested in the deflection of tension cables under load. Price explained:

> As the long span cables are attached to a vertical cantilever in the case of the aviary their ends move inwards due to the deflection of the cantilever and in so doing increase the deflection of the cables, so reducing their tension... the whole acts as a spring.[23]

As built, pretensioned steel cables sheathed in plastic carried the mesh skin of black, anodized and welded aluminium netting. The cables supported an unequal pair of tetrahedrons made of aluminium tubes at either end. Each pair flanked 54-foot (16.5-m), diagonal aluminium shear legs that fixed the skeleton in place. All connections were hinged or pinned to allow for movement.

For Price and Newby the structure was part of the dynamic environment, itself the outcome of a design methodology that required the collaboration of many and adapted to the many challenging inputs encountered in the proposal, manufacturing and construction process. The intersections of structural conditions with organisms had its architectural equivalent in the intersections of those conditions with material forces. One such juncture that took months to solve was how to attach the soft aluminium mesh to the steel cables that carried it in such a way that would allow free rotation so as not to transfer load as would happen with a simple crimped connection. In the end, the mesh was connected to edge stiffeners that were then fixed to the cables by stainless steel links at regular intervals.[24] The cage, itself a system of structural equilibrium, maintained through a variety of controls an ecological system within a larger system of controlled environments, the London Zoo, itself part of a larger urban organism.

The aviary, then, was a system through which the many independent systems, including architectural technology, biological function, ecological milieu and zoological criteria, were integrated. Architecture

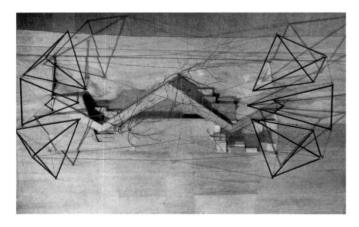

Aluminium structure of the aviary

View of the model of the aviary

Aviary under construction

25   From 'Technology Is the Answer, But What Is the Question?', a lecture was recorded in January of 1979.

26   See Omar Khan and Philip Beesley, *Situated Technologies Pamphlets 4: Responsive Architecture, Performing Instruments* (New York: Architecture League of New York, 2009).

27   For further elaboration, see Bernard Scott, 'Second-order Cybernetics: An Historical Introduction', *Kybernetes* 33/9-10 (2004), 1365-1378.

28   'Technology Is the Answer', op. cit. (note 25).

thus played a role akin to the one that the natural environment had performed for Gilbert White. Ecologies, though, are the products of duration; zoological pavilions do not have that luxury. Instead of time, they have architecture – as Price defined it, architecture is: 'That which, through natural distortion of time, place and interval, creates beneficial social conditions that hitherto were considered impossible.'[25] Thus architecture was positioned as an environmental intervention that allowed for the self-organizing system of the constructed habitat to adapt. For Price, the role of the architect was the orchestration of all levels of information, including those in which the process would register publicly. The aviary, with its figurehead of a playboy married into royalty, insured access to the popular as well as professional media to which Price provided calculated leaks – thus his characteristically extreme reactions to any press that he did not authorize. The composition of the design team also allowed for a blurred stance on authorship. Even the official title, waffling as it did between the Snowdon and Northern Aviary, remained fuzzy.

These fluid components suited the unstable form of the object, too, which for all its orchestration existed in the mind's eye as components that eluded coherence – a feature that is especially clear when looking at other propositions by Price, such as the Fun Palace or Potteries Thinkbelt, in which the work truly does not have a final form.[26] The notion of architecture not as a set of forms, but as a technological procedure, came to Price via a particular understanding of the organizational methodology that has become known as second-order cybernetics – the study of systems that study systems. Cybernetics as a discipline was concerned from the outset with the steering of information in biological, social and mechanical systems. It was a tool that enabled interdisciplinary discourse by providing a shared language through which to interpret the constraints imposed by disciplinary models.[27]

Price's introduction to cybernetic thinking came to him via lectures delivered at the Architectural Association by cybernetician Gordon Pask. Pask was explicit in defining the architect as a mediator of systems, and collaborated with Price on the Fun Palace project during the years that the Aviary was underway and was a frequent visitor to Price's office. One of the hallmarks of the work of Pask and his likeminded colleagues was that they sought to define information not as a quantifiable entity, but instead as a kind of external energy whose perturbations qualitatively registered in a subject. If the first stage of cybernetics was to provide an epistemology for the study of objects, for those who became known as cyberneticians of the second order the system itself was the subject of

investigation. As such, if in the first stage, objects were comprehended in terms of their systems, in the second stage the observer of the system was also understood as a system coming to terms with other systems. In other words, systems observe systems. There are no observer-to-object relationships but only observer-to-observer ones. Systems, if they are truly self-organizing and able to accommodate complexity, will always expand unexpectedly beyond the initial frame of reference.

In the methodology of Price, observers and their unpredictability provide the 'noisy data' over which the system has no predictive powers. Indeterminacy and enabling, two terms associated in the architectural literature with Price, are also tied to second-order cybernetic theory in which underspecified systems require the engagement of observers to complete them. As Price said when remarking on the aviary in a lecture entitled 'Technology Is the Answer, But What Is the Question?':

> Increasingly architecture must be concerned with mixing unknown emotions and responses, or at least enabling such unknowns to work together happily. It is beyond the art of the behavioural scientist to predict all the reactions of the users, whether they be human or animal, within any particular structure. Therefore architecture must be sufficiently accurate to enable this element of doubt and change to be contained.[28]

Habitat for Price was not a replica of place, but a site that harboured the interactions of all shades of participants, not just the human patterns of association. As such, Price was essentially unconcerned with aesthetic cohesiveness because meaning for him did not reside in the qualities of an object per se, but was continually constructed through the varied perceptions of those who engage it. The work was left open to be completed by its users. Thus, the abstraction of the 'natural' features of the habitat was not a formalist gesture, but part of a framework that allows interaction to happen. Cliff, ramp, plants and cage represent no particular known or imagined habitat, but a habitat waiting to be.

PSYCHO-ANALYSIS OF THE DELTA LANDSCAPE

Maps by Pjotr Gonggrijp

Pjotr Gonggrijp (1935) studied architecture at Delft University of Technology. Initially, he worked as a student assistant for Cornelis van Eesteren, the former secretary general of CIAM and mastermind behind Amsterdam's General Extension Plan, and a professor in Delft. Gonggrijp admired as well as criticized Van Eesteren's analytical urban planning doctrine. He found a kindred spirit in Aldo van Eyck, whose imaginative use of language and humanist approach to the experience of architectural space greatly inspired him. After Van Eyck came to teach in Delft, Gonggrijp worked as his teaching assistant for several years.

Gonggrijp graduated in 1969 on a landscape study of the western part of the Netherlands. His design research focused on the ongoing expansion of the Port of Rotterdam, including the location of new docks, the flow of goods and the residential areas in the region. He conducted his studies through a series of large hand-drawn maps, overlaid with multiple transparent sheets to show and analyse the different cultural layers that are superimposed on the landscape.

The drawings involved an analysis of the Dutch delta and its characteristic geological landscape formations in relation to the different settlement patterns. Gonggrijp used various cartographic sources, including contemporary Michelin maps, topographical maps from around 1850 and historical maps by cartographer Jacob van Deventer from the sixteenth century. As a result, his maps often show multiple historical situations at the same time – historical landscapes and cities feature next to the modern infrastructure of docks and railways.

Over the years, Gonggrijp developed a profound fascination for anthropology and psychoanalysis to understand human interaction and organization. From this it becomes clear that the drawings were not only a spatio-architectural tool, but also a means to grasp the specific identity of the landscape and its inhabitants. He sought to trace how habitation patterns also constituted and formed the lived experience of their inhabitants. Scale is an essential tool, from mapping the pattern of small farmyards behind the dunes to the flow of rivers coming from the German and Belgium hinterland, up to the formation of metropolitan areas around the North Sea basin.

His research also included studies into the migration and habitation patterns of birds and humans, or the way pollution spreads under different meteorological circumstances.

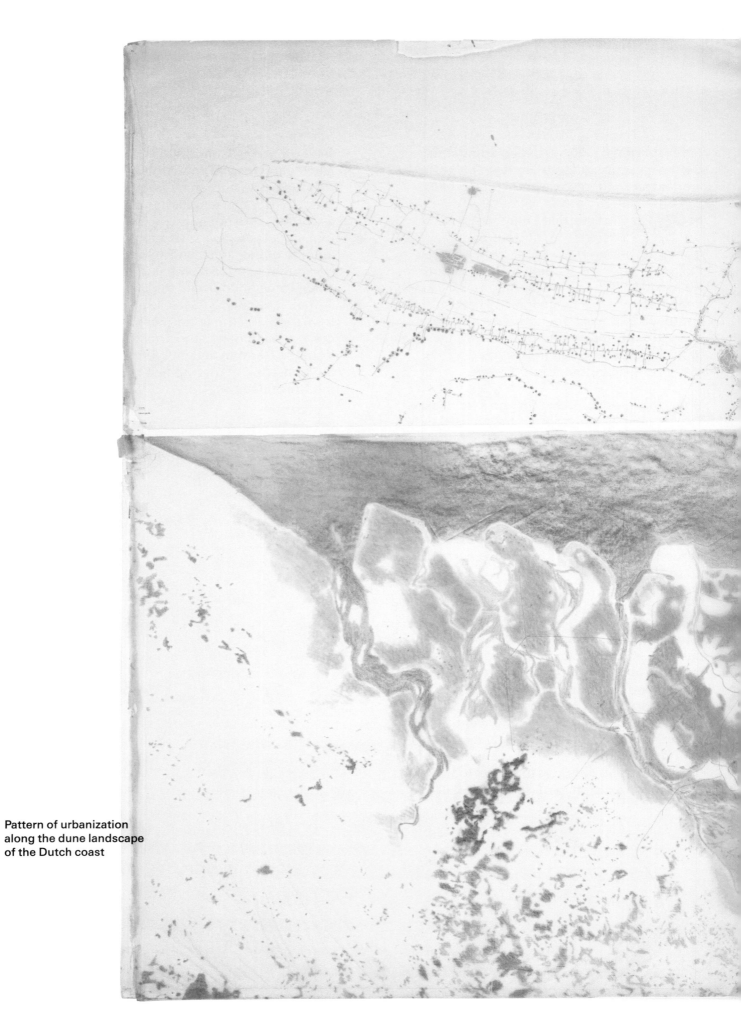

**Pattern of urbanization
along the dune landscape
of the Dutch coast**

Psycho-analysis of the Delta Landscape

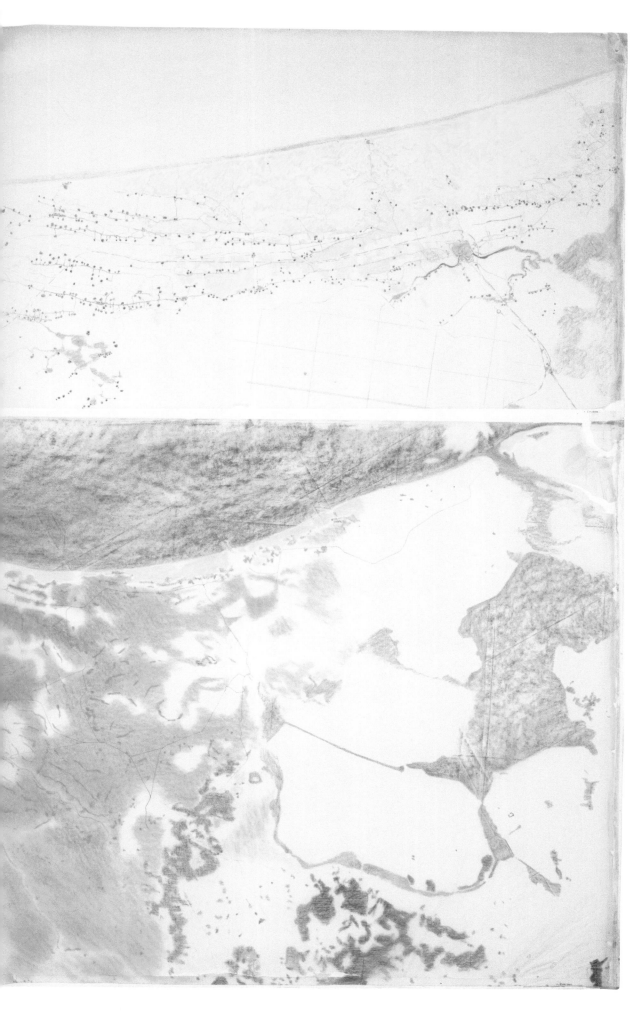

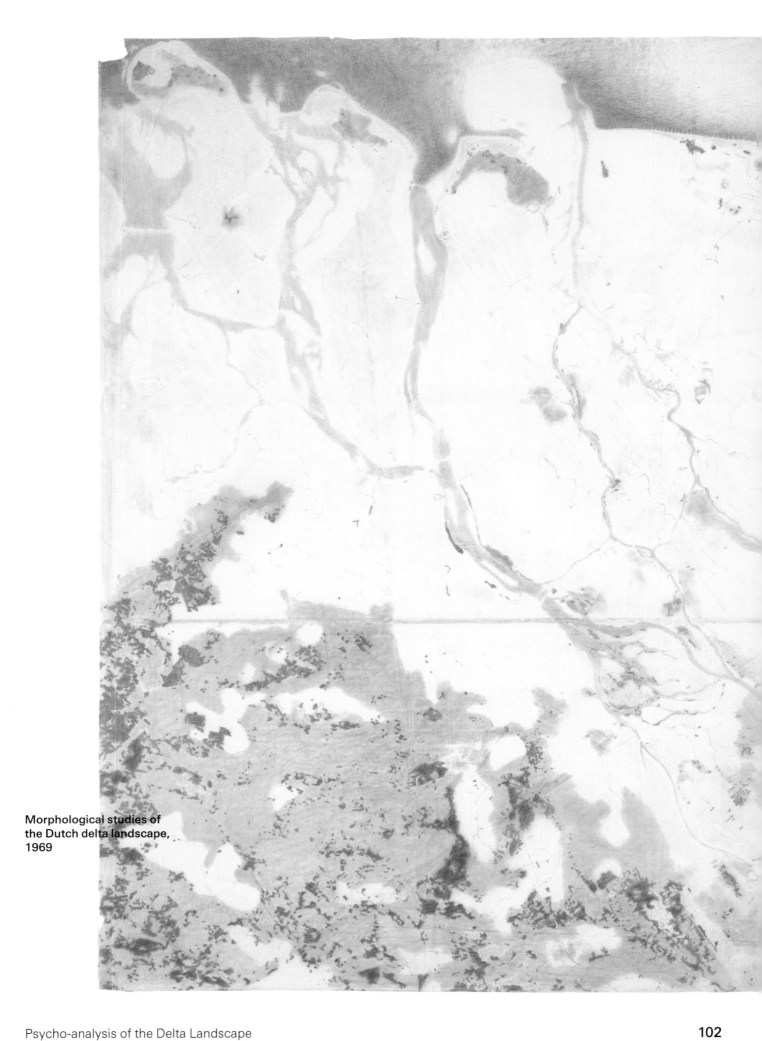

Morphological studies of
the Dutch delta landscape,
1969

Pjotr Gonggrijp

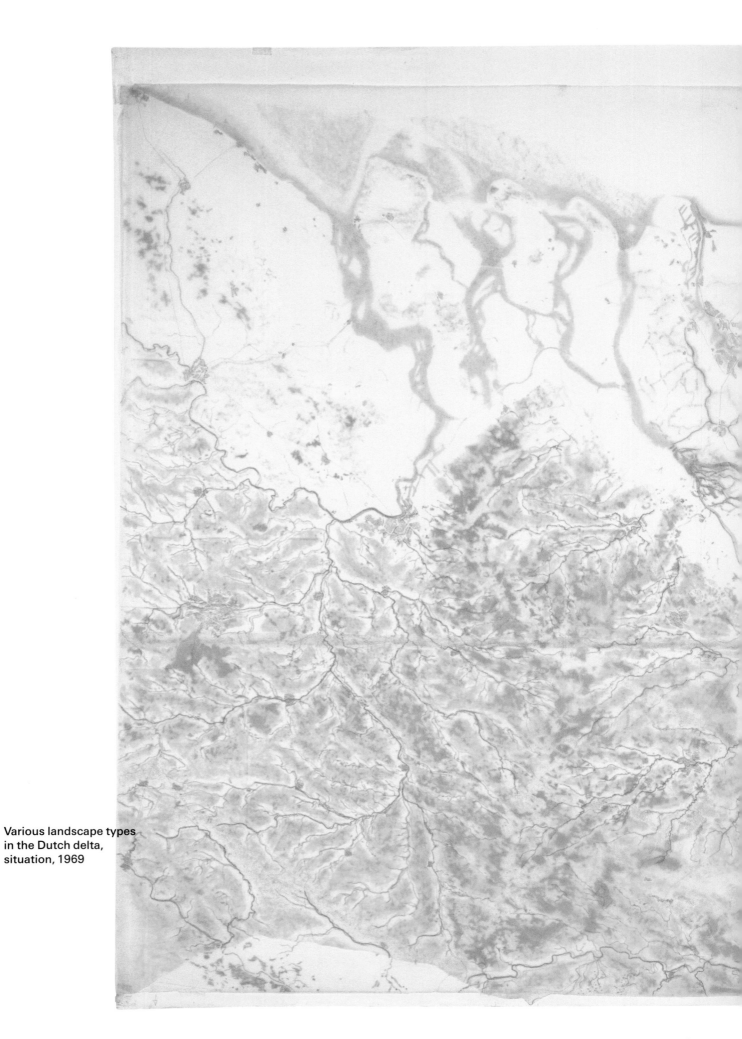

**Various landscape types
in the Dutch delta,
situation, 1969**

Psycho-analysis of the Delta Landscape

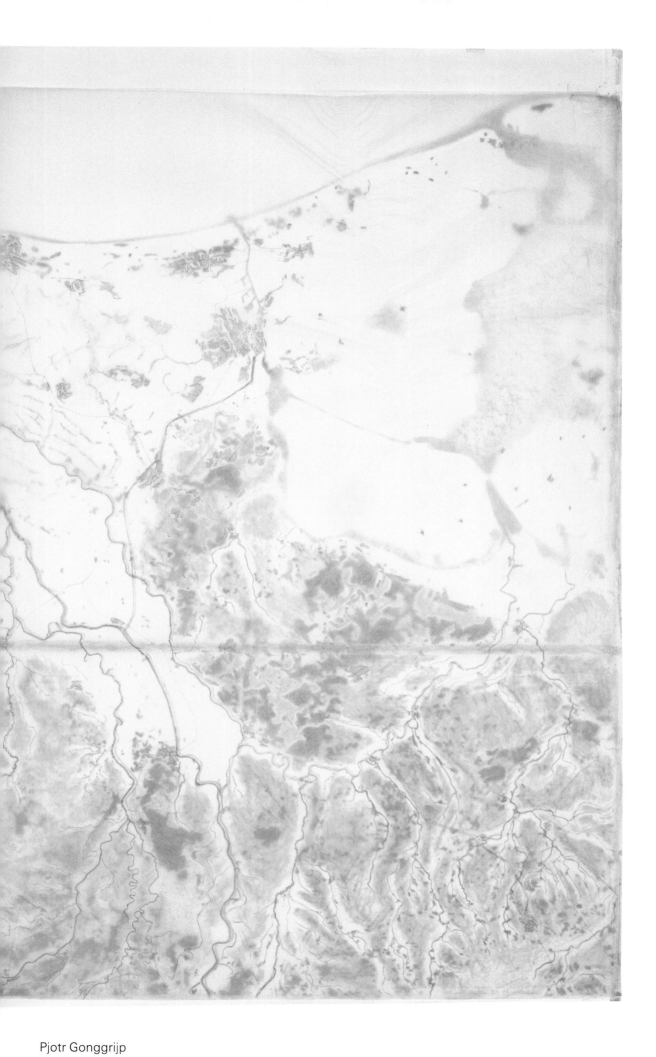

Pjotr Gonggrijp

Situation and proposals for
urbanization of the deltas
of Hamburg, Rotterdam
and London (showing the
MARS plan), 1969

Various landscape types
in Noord-Brabant with the
Biesbosch wetlands, and
the cities of Geertruidenberg
and Breda

The islands of Walcheren
and Noord- and Zuid-
Beveland in the province
of Zeeland, with the cities
of Middelburg and Goes

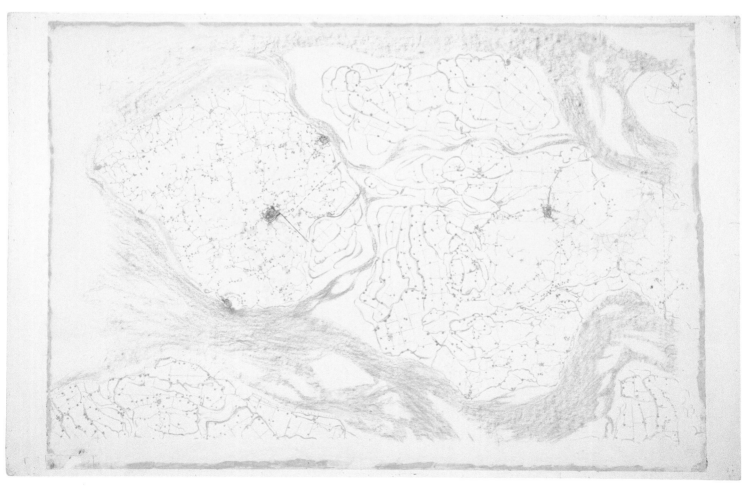

Pjotr Gonggrijp

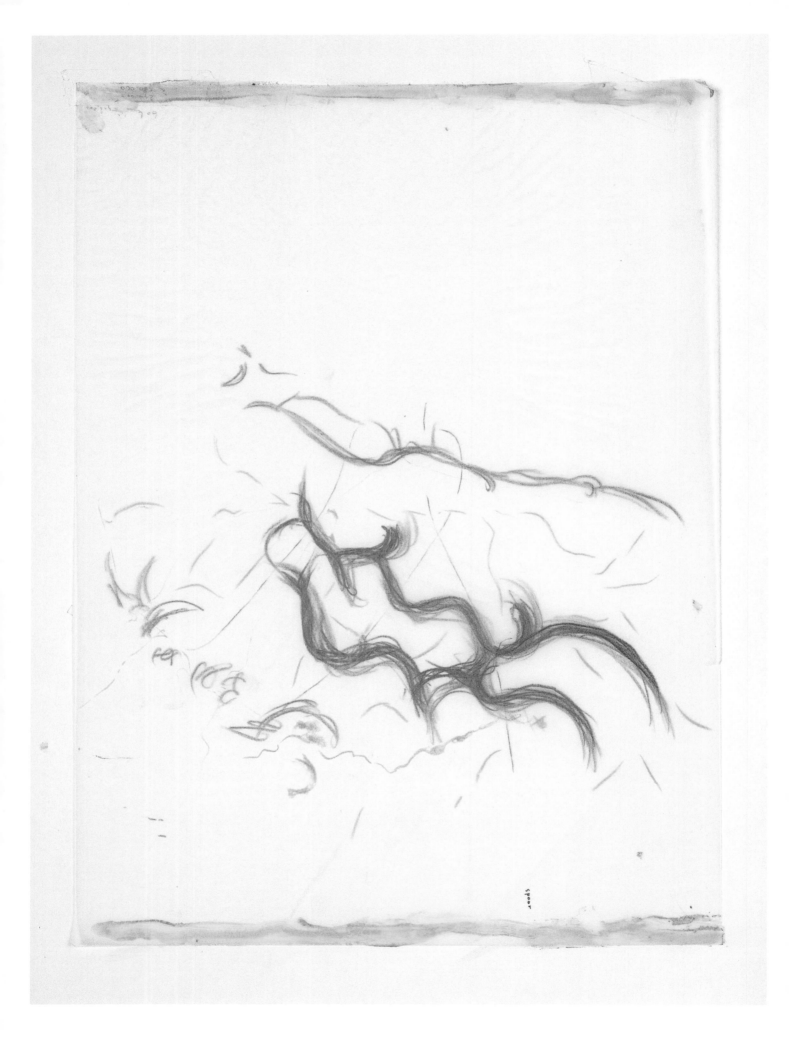

Psycho-analysis of the Delta Landscape

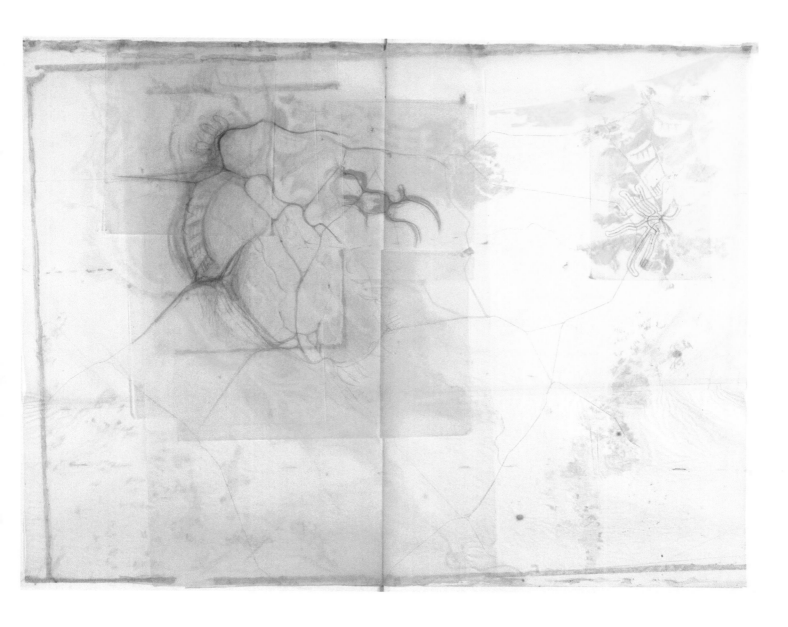

Study for the large-scale
urbanization in the province
of Zuid-Holland, 1969

Pjotr Gonggrijp

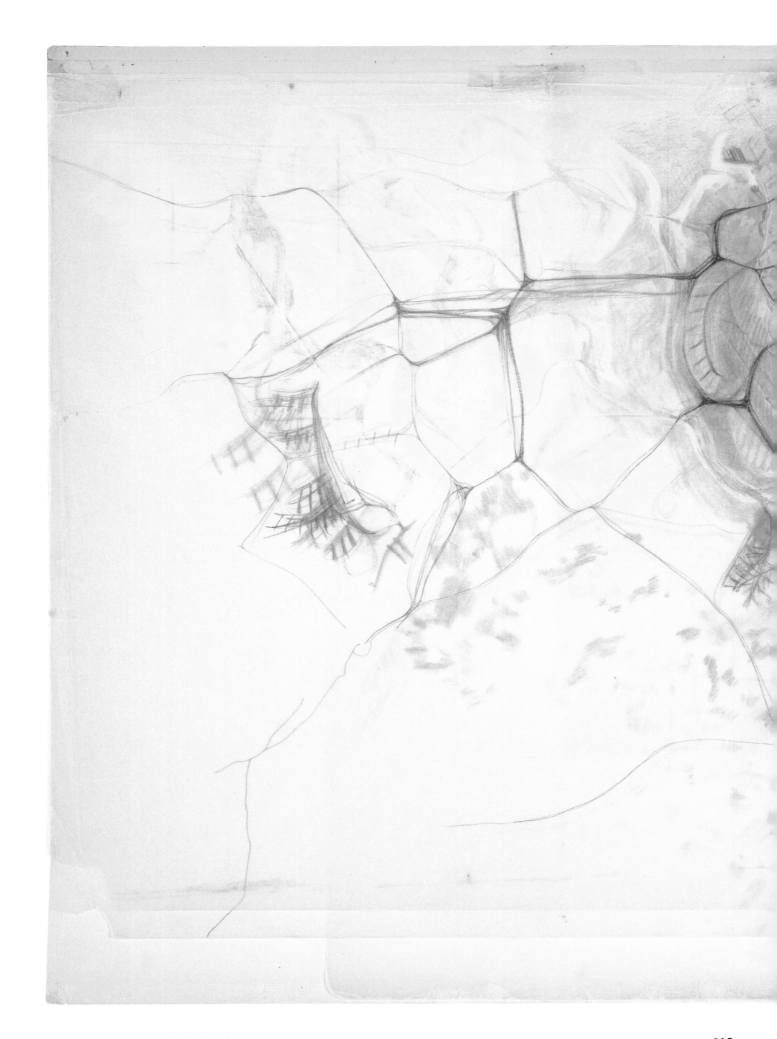

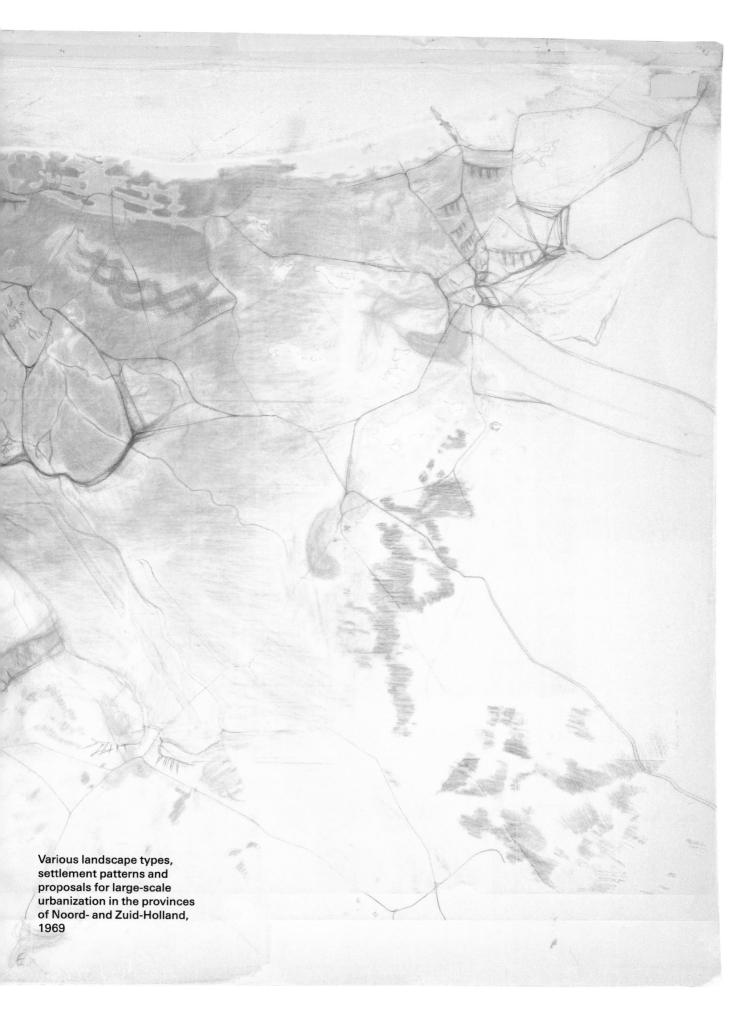

Various landscape types,
settlement patterns and
proposals for large-scale
urbanization in the provinces
of Noord- and Zuid-Holland,
1969

Pjotr Gonggrijp

Psycho-analysis of the Delta Landscape

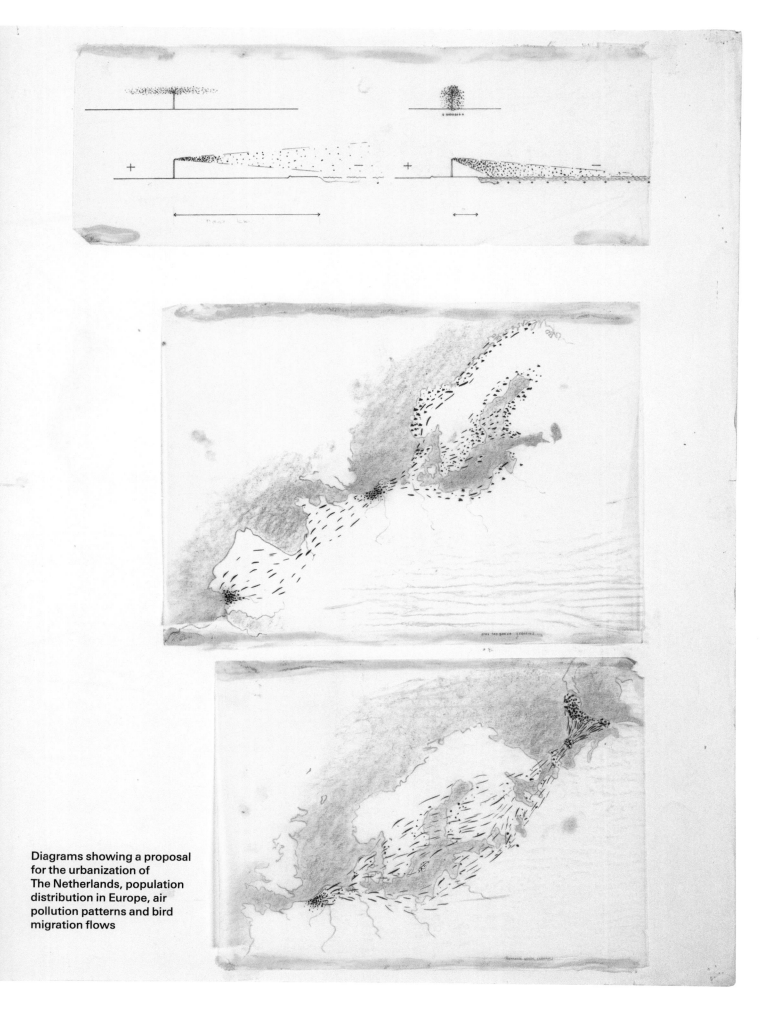

Diagrams showing a proposal
for the urbanization of
The Netherlands, population
distribution in Europe, air
pollution patterns and bird
migration flows

Pjotr Gonggrijp

TANTHOF DELFT

Designs by Van den Broek and Bakema,
Tanthof Working Group and Joost Váhl

The initial design for Tanthof, a residential area south of Delft, was made by the Rotterdam office of Van den Broek and Bakema in 1969. The plan provides a core of high-rise slabs along and over a major trunk road towards Rotterdam, with the low-rise neighbourhoods situated around it, in accordance with the formal, typological and organizational characteristics of the firm's modernist principles. However, this plan was rejected by the city after criticism from a group of activists and recently graduated Delft architecture students who called for a more contextual and ecological approach. The trunk road disappeared, as did the high-rise developments. In line with the egalitarian government models of the 1970s, a broad working group was created to concoct a new plan. Thijs de Jong, head of the Department of Public Works of Delft, facilitated this new process. Municipal employees and residents' representatives worked together with designers from Van den Broek and Bakema to incorporate the critique on the first design into a new proposal, among those Anneloes van de Berg, Hiwe Groenewolt, Sjirk Haaksma, Frans Hooykaas, and Peter Lüthi. Frans Hooykaas, together with Jan Stokla and Abe Bonnema, worked on the housing scheme that was eventually realized by Van den Broek and Bakema.

Among the members of the working group was urban planner Joost Váhl (1939), who had been one of the first to argue for the curbing of motorized traffic in domestic areas; he has been credited with installing the world's first speed bump, and lauded as the inventor of the *woonerf* (low- and mixed-traffic residential areas). He was critical of the monotonous built and natural environments that 1960s neighbourhoods represented. Váhl proposed more urban diversity, both by combining traffic flows of cars, bicycles and pedestrians and through realizing a more varied urban flora and fauna through simple landscaping measures such as water features, height differences or planting weeds.

The working group developed an entirely new plan that clearly bears the mark of Váhl's approach. Instead of disappearing under a metres-thick layer of sand, as was customary in the construction of residential areas in the polders of Holland, the existing landscape now forms the basis for the new design. The historical hamlet of Abtswoude and its farms is the central linear element. Housing and car access are integrated with waterways and a network for pedestrians and cyclists, with various architecture firms called in to work on the design of the residential neighbourhoods.

Van den Broek and Bakema realized one of the southern neighbourhoods (1975-1981), arranging the houses based on a historical farmyard pattern where the buildings are grouped together around the yard, while bringing canals into the neighbourhood. The architectural vernacular with picturesque sloping roofs and the mixed use of wood and concrete brick represents a drastic change in comparison with the initial proposal, and recalls the holiday parks the firm previously designed for Sporthuis Centrum.

Polder landscape prior
to the construction of
the Tanthof, c. 1971

Projection of the old town
of Delft on the Tanthof site,
to give an idea of size and
distance, 1972

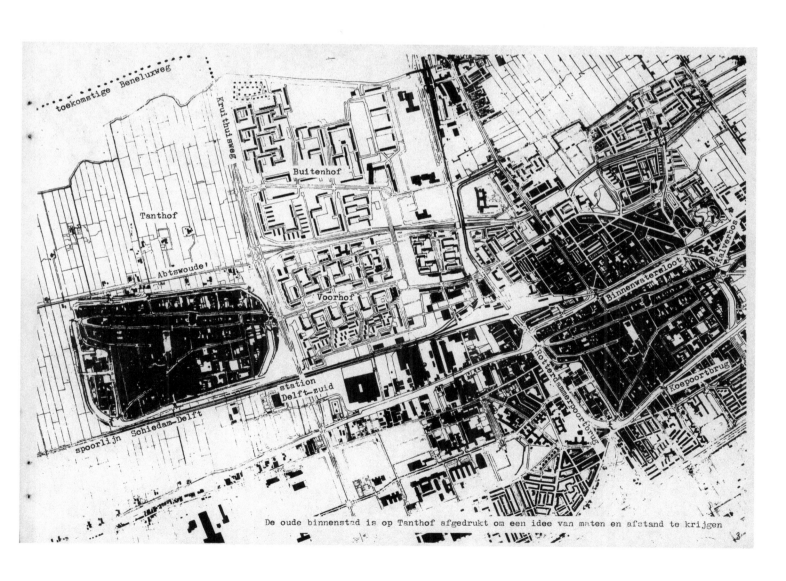

De oude binnenstad is op Tanthof afgedrukt om een idee van maten en afstand te krijgen

Van den Broek and Bakema,
Tanthof Working Group, Joost Váhl

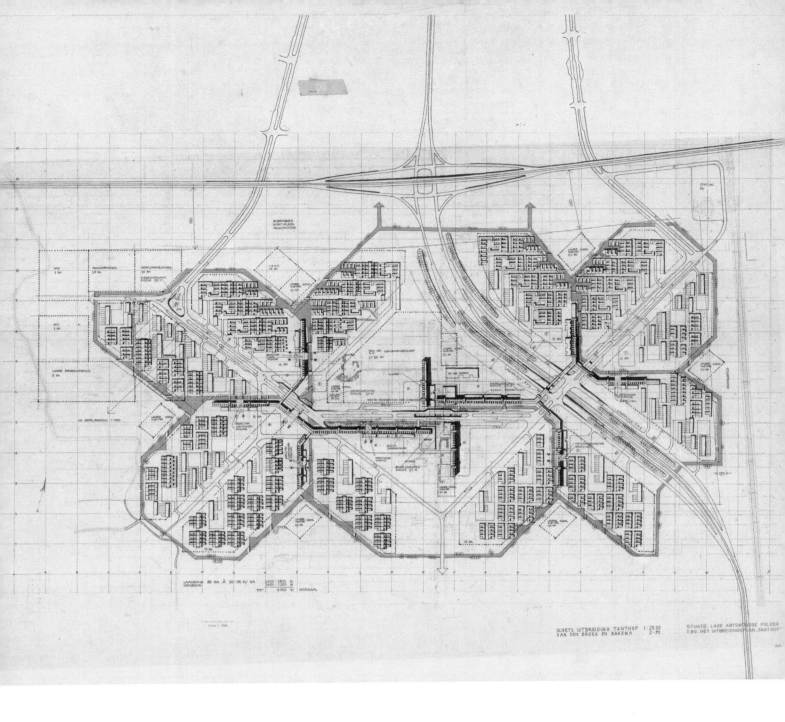

Van den Broek and Bakema

Urban plan Tanthof, Delft,
first version, 1969

Department of Public Works
of Delft, Joost Váhl

'Analysis of the design of
Van den Broek and Bakema:
Suggestions for a Better
Plan', 1971

Proposal for a 'less
pronounced and much
simpler' network grid for
Tanthof, 1971

Plan matching the structure
of the proposed development
with that of the existing
landscape and farmsteads,
1971

Tanthof Delft

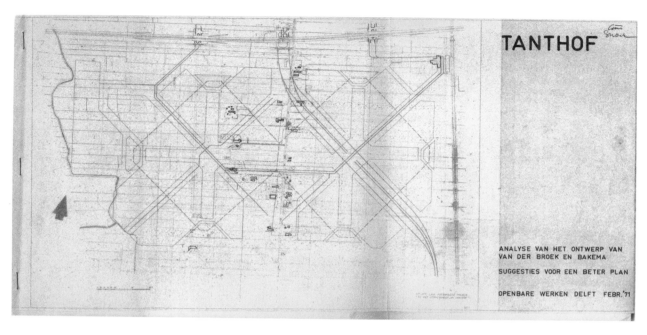

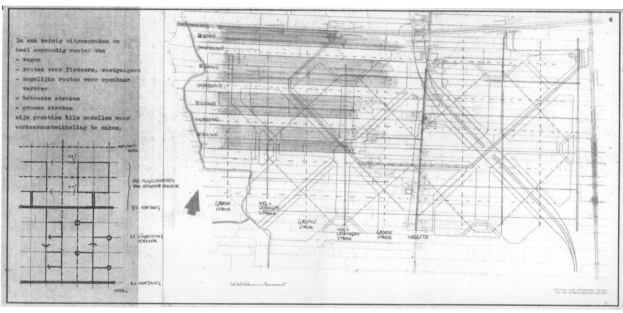

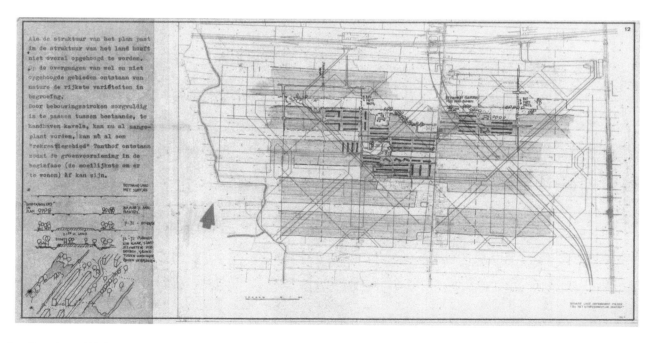

Van den Broek and Bakema,
Tanthof Working Group, Joost Váhl

Jaap Bakema

Density studies for Tanthof
Delft, second urban plan,
c. 1970

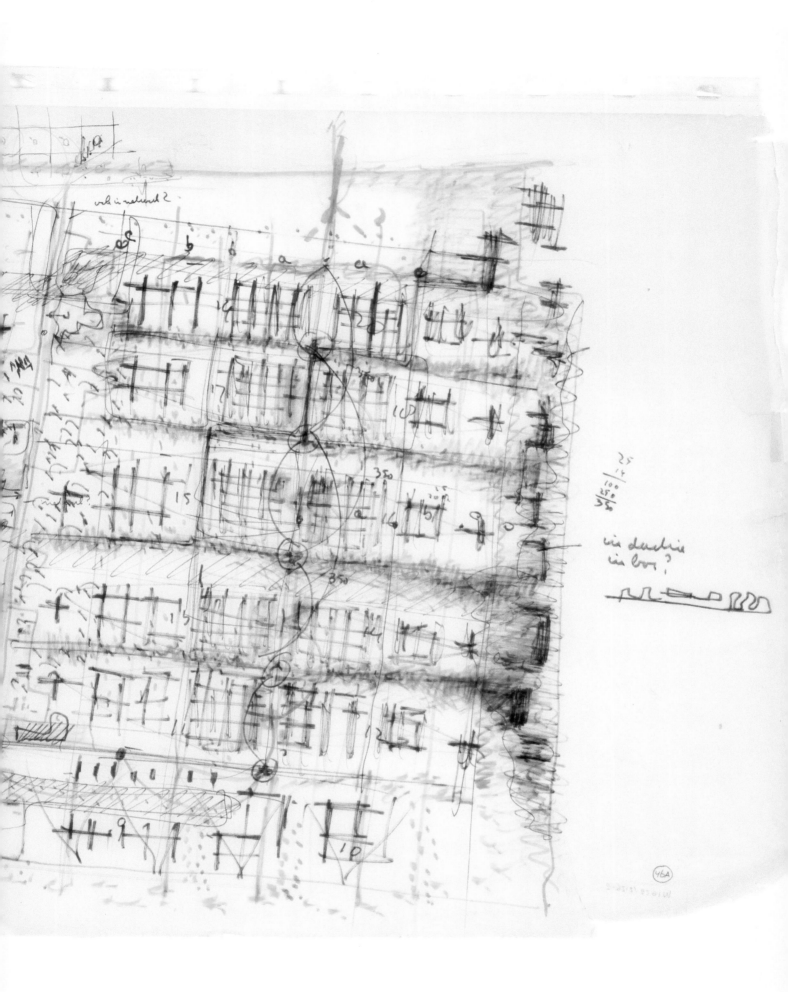

Van den Broek and Bakema,
Tanthof Working Group, Joost Váhl

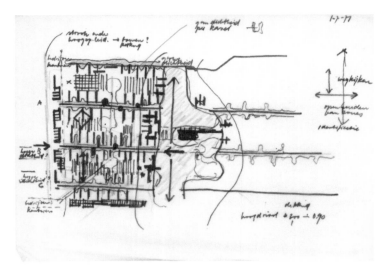

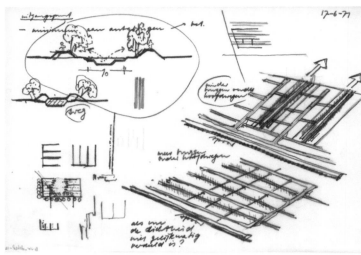

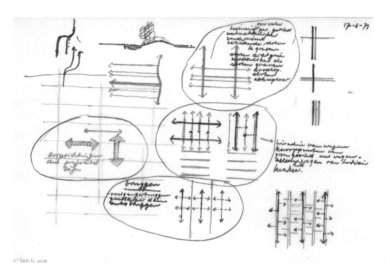

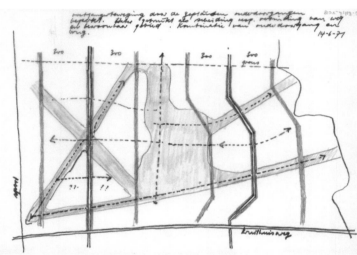

Tanthof Working Group
Drawings by Peter Lüthi

Study of the integration
of urban and landscape
structures, 1971

Study of the integration
of water system, green
structure, pedestrian routes
and car traffic, 1971

Study of the integration of
landscape structures, depth
of housing blocks and road
infrastructure, 1971

Study of the integration
landscape structures and
walking paths, 1971

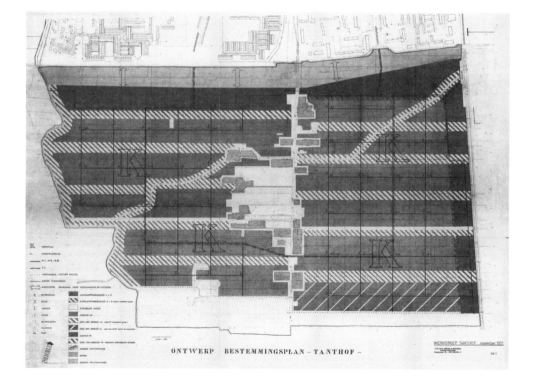

Tanthof Working Group

Cover of 'Tanthof:
Explanation of the Zoning
Plan', 1972

Zoning plan of Tanthof,
based on the existing
landscape structures, 1971

Van den Broek and Bakema,
Tanthof Working Group, Joost Váhl

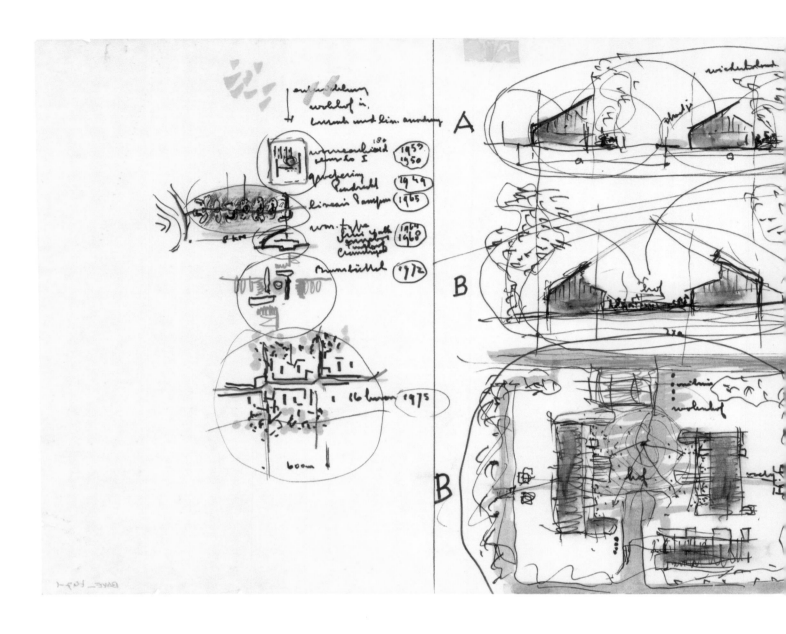

Jaap Bakema

Study for a residential cluster
around a yard, including
a timeline of housing unit
typologies

Jaap Bakema, Hiwe
Groenewolt and Peter
Lüthi on an excursion to
Vennenbos holiday park,
Hapert

View of the model of a
housing cluster inspired
by a farm yard, second
version of the plan, 1975

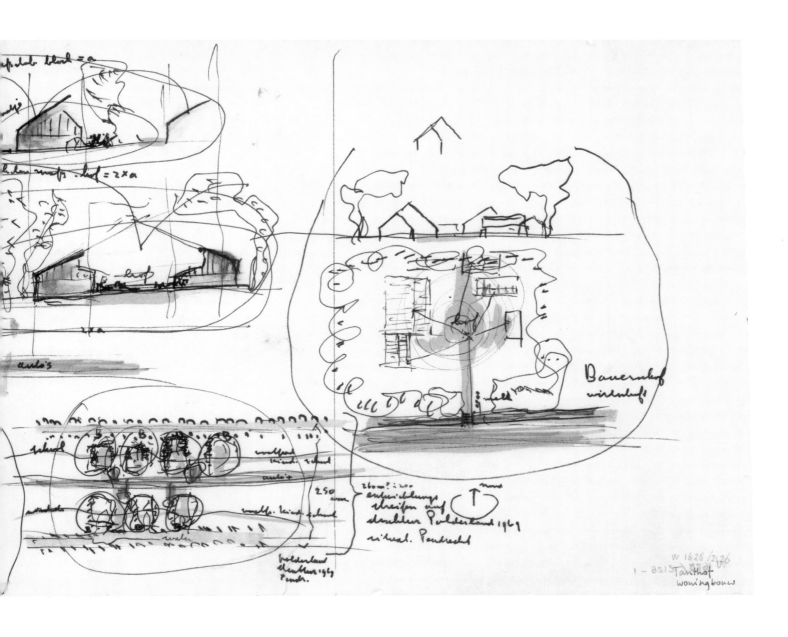

Van den Broek and Bakema,
Tanthof Working Group, Joost Váhl

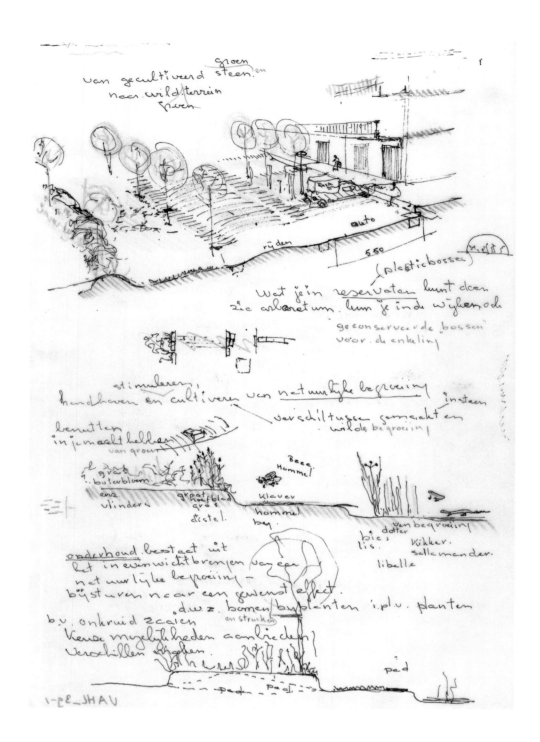

Joost Váhl

Sketches and notes on the relationship between city and landscape, 1970-1972

Joost Váhl

Various notes and sketches on the relationship between city and landscape, dwelling and planting, vegetation and the experience of waterfronts, 1970-1972

Van den Broek and Bakema

Tanthof residential neighbourhood, integrating water, parking, and low rise housing, 1981

Beschutting
en intimiteit

—ook in de nieuwbouw

A

wilgenstaak   ruggetje

A¹

els+wilg 1e jaar al   kruiden gezaaid

B

Koolzaad
lupine
springbalsemien
enz.

palen + b.v. kippegaas, bonen
hop of bruidsluier e.d. ertegen
laten groeien.

B¹

jonge aanplant +
bruidsluier

na 1e seizoen

VÁHL

VLAK BIJ HUIS

men kan een terrein plat
maken

erop
eruit

maar ook hobbelig voor het-
zelfde geld.

vlak ingezaaid met gras

men kan ook kruiden zaaien.

gebruik nivoverschillen én
kruiden én jonge aanplant om
al het eerste seizoen her-
bergzame plekken te maken.

regelmatig
maaien én
ingezaaid met kruiden
geeft meer gebruikswaar-
den.

VÁHL

Van den Broek and Bakema,
Tanthof Working Group, Joost Váhl

Erik Rietveld and Janno Martens

ARCHITECTURE AND ECOLOGICAL PSYCHOLOGY

RAAAF's Explorations of Affordances

RAAAF and Atelier de Lyon,
Bunker 599, Culemborg, 2013

1   James Jerome Gibson, *The Ecological Approach to Visual Perception* (Boston: Houghton Mifflin Harcourt, 1979), 140.
2   Erik Rietveld, *Unreflective Action: A Philosophical Contribution to Integrative Neuroscience* (Amsterdam: ILLC Dissertation Series, 2008); and Erik Rietveld, 'Situated Normativity: the Normative Aspect of Embodied Cognition in Unreflective Action', in *Mind* 177/468 (2008), 973-1001.
3   Rietveld's work at the University of Amsterdam has been supported by NWO VENI and VIDI grants, as well as an ERC Starting Grant. For more about Rietveld's research, see www.erikrietveld.com.

4   Gibson, *The Ecological Approach,* op. cit. (note 1), 127-128.
5   This is based on Wittgenstein's notion of *feste Lebensformen*, see Ludwig Wittgenstein, 'Cause and Effect: Intuitive Awareness', in: James Carl Klagge and Alfred Nordmann (eds.), *Philosophical Occasions 1912-1951* (Indianapolis: Hackett, 1993), 397.
6   Gibson, *The Ecological Approach,* op. cit. (note 1), 137.
7   Erik Rietveld and Julian Kiverstein, 'A Rich Landscape of Affordances', *Ecological Psychology* 26/4 (2014), 235-352.

The perceiving of an affordance is... a process of perceiving a value-rich ecological object. Any substance, any surface, any layout has some affordance for benefit or injury to someone. Physics may be value-free, but ecology is not.
— James Gibson [1]

One of the themes behind habitat is the notion that the built environment should not be understood as a collection of static objects, but as a dynamic or ecological system, thus introducing a process-based and relational approach to architecture and planning. This view is a cornerstone of the work of RAAAF [Rietveld Architecture-Art-Affordances], a studio founded by architect Ronald Rietveld and philosopher Erik Rietveld in 2006 that operates at the crossroads of visual art, architecture and philosophy. RAAAF makes architectural installations, interventions and works of art that question practices in our contemporary living environment. These practices range from everyday entrenched habits such as sitting too much to issues of social cohesion and public space to institutional conservation practices or the temporary use of vacant buildings. Through a working method based on multidisciplinary research conducted with scientists and other specialists, these real-life thinking models link local qualities with long-term strategies aimed at influencing societal, social or institutional developments. As the name suggests, RAAAF's installations create *affordances*, a concept from ecological psychology that signifies possibilities for action provided by the environment. In parallel and in conjunction with the work of RAAAF, Erik Rietveld's research group at the University of Amsterdam has been investigating this notion for over a decade. Based on earlier philosophical work on skilled action,[2] this ongoing research project explores how affordances can be relevant not just to the fields of philosophy and psychology, but also to cognitive science, psychiatry and architecture.[3] The way RAAAF employs the concept of affordances for its interventions can serve as an inspiring contemporary example of an approach to architecture that no longer thinks in terms of objects, form and construction, but rather in terms of processes, systems and ecological niches.

Ecological Psychology and the Rich Landscape of Affordances

The notion of affordances was introduced by ecological psychologist James Gibson, who was among the first to stress the importance of our environment and its perception to the field of psychology. Affordances are possibilities for action provided to an animal (including humans) by the environment: by the substances, surfaces, objects and other living creatures that surround the animal. Generalizing somewhat, we can say, for example, that surfaces afford locomotion and support, substances afford nutrition and manufacture, objects afford manipulation, other animals afford a variety of interactions and other people afford, as Gibson put it, 'the whole spectrum of social significance'.[4] What is common to human beings is not just the biology we share but also how we are embedded in sociocultural practices: our relatively stable shared ways of getting on and living with others that we, following Austrian philosopher Ludwig Wittgenstein, have called the human form of life.[5]

Each species of animal has its own distinctive form of life, which is reflected in Gibson's definition of the concept of an ecological niche. For Gibson, an ecological niche is built and transformed by members of the species through their patterns of behaviours. All animals actively modify their niches, tailoring the places they inhabit to match their needs – from nests, holes, burrows, paths and webs all the way up to squares, streets, houses and cities. Note the materiality of the environment that offers affordances: the organism alters the material environment in order that the latter offers possibilities for action that may improve the organism's situation. But an ecological niche is not just material: it is best seen as an evolving process of interconnected affordances available in a particular form of life on the basis of the abilities manifested in its collective practices – its relatively stable ways of doing things. An individual affordance is an aspect of such an ecological niche, and each affordance must be understood in relation to the abilities available in a form of life.

Some human abilities are shared by all of us; others are not, because we participate in different sociocultural practices. Gibson has pointed out that 'at the highest level, when vocalization becomes speech and human manufactured displays become images, pictures and writing, the affordances of human behaviour are staggering'.[6] Traditionally, affordances have been understood primarily as a concept applied to 'lower' motor cognition such as grasping a cup or riding a bike. However, within the framework developed at the University of Amsterdam, we have proposed thinking of 'higher' cognitive capacities as well, in terms of skilled activities in sociocultural practices in relation to the material resources available in those practices.[7] Both 'lower' motor cognition and skilled 'higher' cognition can thus be equally understood in terms of a situated and selective engagement with a rich landscape of affordances.

In order to do justice to this relationship with our ecological niche and its potential for our understanding

RAAAF and Barbara Visser,
The End of Sitting, **Amsterdam,**
2014

Erik Rietveld testing positions
in a mock-up for *The End of*
Sitting

8   For more about the notion
of *sociomateriality*, which holds
that the material and the social
aspects of our environment are
entangled and cannot be clearly
separated, see Ludger van Dijk
and Erik Rietveld, 'Foregrounding
Sociomaterial Practice in Our
Understanding of Affordances:
The Skilled Intentionality
Framework', *Frontiers in Psychology*
7 (2017); and Ludger van Dijk
and Erik Rietveld, 'Situated
Anticipation', *Synthese* (2018).
9   Ronald Rietveld and Erik
Rietveld, *Dutch Atlas of Vacancy*
(Rotterdam: NAi Publishers, 2010);
Erik Rietveld and Ronald Rietveld,
'The Dutch Atlas of Vacancy', in:
Ronald Rietveld and Erik Rietveld
(eds.), *Vacancy Studies: Experiments*
and Strategic Interventions in
Architecture (Rotterdam, nai010
publishers, 2015), 51-78.

10   Van Dijk and Rietveld,
'Foregrounding Sociomaterial
Practice', op. cit. (note 8).
11   The theoretical background
of social affordances in relation
to this project are elaborated in
Erik Rietveld, Ronald Ronald and
Janno Martens, 'Trusted Strangers:
Social Affordances for Social
Cohesion', *Phenomenology and*
the Cognitive Sciences 18/1 (2019),
299-316.

of so-called 'higher' cognition, our research group has defined affordances as relationships between aspects of the sociomaterial environment in flux and abilities available in a form of life.[8] In the case of humans, these available abilities are generally acquired through training and experience in sociocultural practices. Our ecological niche is therefore much richer than many might have supposed, including the vast amount of possibilities offered by complex skills such as reasoning, language use and advanced social functions. Having a better conceptual understanding of the relational nature of affordances is vital to creative professions, because it suggests new ways of increasing our openness to underutilized affordances.

RAAAF demonstrated an architectural application of this principle in the exhibition 'Vacant NL', in the Dutch pavilion at the 2010 Venice Architecture Biennale, emphasizing the potential of the affordances offered by vacant buildings in the Netherlands. The affordances they presented should be seen as relationships between the variety of the physical structures (older buildings, often built for very specific purposes) and the diverse repertoire of human abilities. 'Vacant NL' explored the qualitative aspects of vacancy and revealed the extremely rich 'nests' of resources these buildings represent.[9] In the Netherlands there are thousands of vacant buildings – not just offices, but, crucially, many unique structures with a great variety of spatial qualities as well, since they were once designed for specific purposes: lighthouses, hospitals, water towers, factories, airports, hangars, offices, rehabilitation centres, fortresses, bunkers, schools, swimming pools and so many others. All of these buildings were constructed at times when function, craftsmanship and the use of materials were approached differently than today, which renders many of them non-reproducible. Their diversity and unique properties distinguish them from the generic spaces of vacant contemporary office space and present irreplaceable possibilities for action – affordances – that will invite unexpected experimentation were this reservoir of resources unlocked. A vacant school, for instance, is a resource-rich place in the landscape of affordances that could be used for many different purposes: as a movie set, for example, a gallery space or a workspace for young app makers.

Architecture and Social Affordances

Since the notion of affordances in our definition extends beyond just physical action and includes the social domain as well, RAAAF has been particularly interested in the design of social affordances. Social affordances are a subcategory of affordances: possibilities for social interaction or sociability provided by the environment. Social affordances can invite social interactions that over time, if engaged in by sufficient numbers of people, may result into transformed patterns of behaviour – that is, into transformed sociocultural practices.[10]

This idea was used as the premise for one of RAAAF's boldest proposals to date, located in Amsterdam. In 2025, Amsterdam will be 750 years old, and the city wants to use this occasion to celebrate its free-thinking heritage. Taking into account the urgent need for good public domain along with our own research into and views on how to create such spaces, RAAAF and Atelier de Lyon responded to this objective by proposing a temporary floating park called *Trusted Strangers | New Amsterdam Park (N.A.P.)*. Along the northern bank of the River IJ and the former dockyard that overlooks Amsterdam's historical city located across the water, a fleet of barges will be docked, forming the basis of the new floating park. A grid of 24 large barges (each 80 m long, 11 m wide and 6 m high) will shelter a hidden water world with an abundance of social affordances.

Twelve of these barges will be temporarily occupied by different sociocultural groups, each allowed to have a barge furnished according to its own preferences. The members of these groups share interests and manifest shared patterns of behaviour, which we broadly defined as 'subcultures' to determine the programme and properties of a specific barge. For example, one barge could accommodate skaters by including halfpipes, spine transfers and banked ramps, while another could be furnished to host bird watchers by incorporating lookouts into the superstructure. This is also the idea behind the other twelve areas of the park, but instead of catering to a specific subculture, the remaining barges provide landscapes of social affordances with a broader appeal: the Campfire Barge, for example, invites the gathering of people who like to be warm (who doesn't?), while the Panna Barge attracts people from different sociocultural groups who like to play soccer. A barge filled with sand dunes has a similar potential: sand is a compelling social affordance where children and parents from different subcultures can meet. Its attractive location and inviting design encourage people to leave their 'own' subcultural barge and join others in a common activity. By accommodating both subcultural niches as well as 'public' activities with a broad appeal, the park becomes a condensed city floating on the water. And because these barges' social affordances are made to be attractive for people with diverse sociocultural backgrounds, they are able to generate new patterns of behaviour and invite surprising spontaneous interactions.[11]

Erik Rietveld and Janno Martens

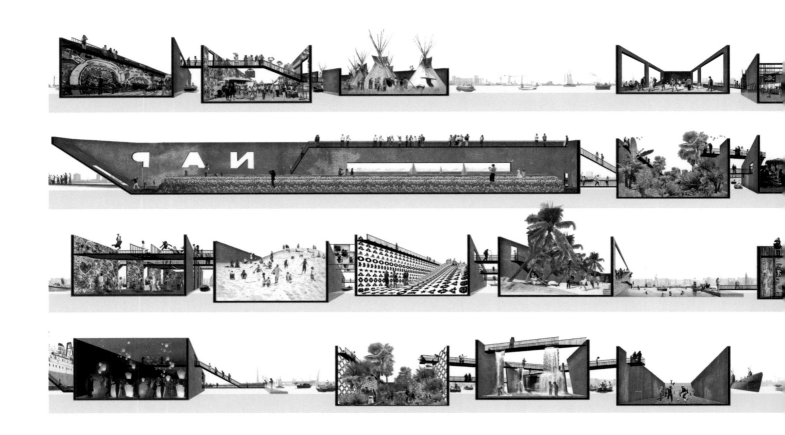

RAAAF and Atelier de Lyon,
N.A.P (New Amsterdam Park),
interior views of the barges
on the IJ river in Amsterdam

RAAAF and Atelier de Lyon,
N.A.P (New Amsterdam Park),
overview of the park

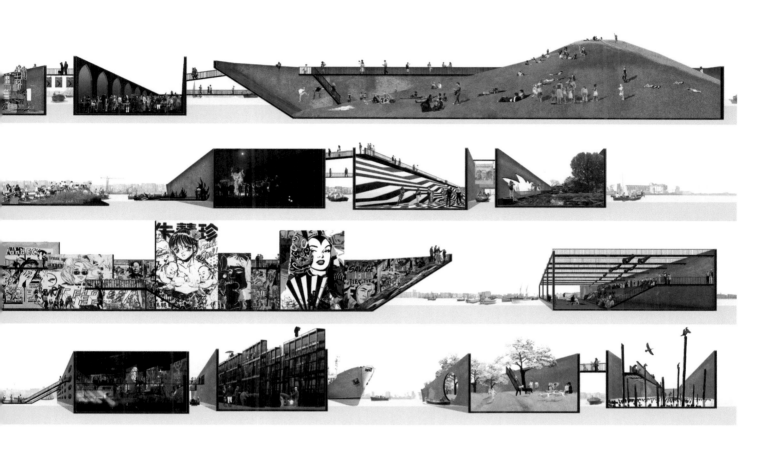

RAAAF, *Breaking Habits*, Amsterdam, 2017

12   Ivan Nio, Arnold Reijndorp and Wouter Velthuis, *Atlas Westelijke Tuinsteden Amsterdam: De geplande en de geleefde stad* (Haarlem: Trancity, 2008), 134; cf. Jane Jacobs, *The Death and Life of Great American Cities* (New York: Random House, 1961).

13   VROM advisory council, *Stad en stijging: Sociale stijging als leidraad voor stedelijke vernieuwing. Advies 054* (The Hague: VROM Advisory Council, 2006), 58.

14   Julian Kiverstein, Mark Miller and Erik Rietveld, 'The Feeling of Grip: Novelty, Error Dynamics and the Predictive Brain', *Synthese* 196/7 (2019), 2847-2869.

15   It should be noted, however, that further research is needed to establish how this finding holds over longer periods of time and with an older population. See Rob Withagen and Simone R. Caljouw, 'The End of Sitting: An Empirical Study on Working in an Office of the Future', *Sports Medicine* 46/7 (2016), 1019-1027.

16   Ibid., 1019.

Familiarity and trust are crucial for the social fabric of the city, and good public spaces are imperative for achieving this. In their study of ethnic and social diversity in Amsterdam's Westelijke Tuinsteden district, authors Ivan Nio, Arnold Reijndorp and Wouter Veldhuis emphasized that this familiarity with others forms the core of well-functioning public spaces. They argue that such spaces foster interactions, and their study underlines the importance of people becoming 'familiar strangers' to their neighbours.[12] This view was echoed in a report from the Dutch advisory council on housing, spatial planning and the environment (VROM-raad), which concluded that a lack of social cohesion is primarily to be understood as a lack of such experienced public familiarity, or, more precisely, as a lack of familiar strangers in the street or neighbourhood.[13] The opportunity to observe groups of 'strangers' and subcultures from a distance is essential to becoming familiar with their ways of doing things in order to become 'trusted familiar strangers'.

This notion of trusted strangers served as the project's premise: observing and being observed is made possible by the material environment (portholes, cut-throughs and the meandering overhead pathways all contribute to this) and is essential to the culture of this park. Sailing through the 'water streets' by boat or walking through the dense labyrinth of barges, staircases, bridges and overhead pathways generates a series of informal encounters, confrontations, exchanges and gatherings. The configuration of the barge grid, combined with routes over water and over the barges, ensures that people cannot simply stick to their familiar surroundings. Due to the changing programme of the twelve barges dedicated to specific groups, visitors will dynamically encounter many different worlds and subcultures.

One of the other key aspects of the *New Amsterdam Park* is that all spaces are to be freely accessible to the public. The open character of the park ensures that visitors can roam freely and over time explore more and more aspects of the park. This opportunity to roam freely is important: as recent work in theoretical computational neuroscience shows, humans display a tendency to gradually explore larger and larger aspects of their ecological niche.[14] This offers a dynamic perspective of how people will appropriate their environment over time, which has been incorporated in the proposal. The architecture of the park is designed in such a way that we expect people, who at first naturally gravitate towards the barge that aligns most with their own interests and subculture, will eventually respond to more and more of the social affordances offered by the park. It should therefore be understood not just as a landscape in the classical physical sense, but also as a rich landscape of social affordances.

Real-Life Thinking Models

As the *N.A.P.* project makes clear, the creation of particular affordances can allow for a change in social patterns, which is something RAAAF incorporates in virtually all of its projects. Some projects, however, like *The End of Sitting* (2014), are also concerned with the less tangible goal of changing the entrenched practices or conventions of our human ecological niche. By showing what the world might look like if our material environment were geared towards entirely different practices from the ones to which we are accustomed, RAAAF offers a reflection on or critique of our current way of doing things – our current form of life. These site-specific interventions are conceived as real-life thinking models that show the potential of an approach that incorporates insights from ecological psychology and the philosophy of affordances in radical interventions and installations that allow for embodied engagement by its visitors and users.

The End of Sitting proposed an alternative vision for the office of the future in which there are no chairs or tables, but that rather consist of a landscape of inclined planes to support different standing and leaning positions, that is, affordances for supported standing or leaning. The art installation accounts for a variety of different body heights and invites people to stand, lean and recline in the context of work, where such physical abilities are not normally used. Now, however, these abilities can be used to take advantage of the affordances provided by this radically different environment. Some of these are deliberately designed possibilities for supported standing, while others are more unorthodox affordances, which can be enacted spontaneously by a person with a relevant skill. In order to arrive at the spatial particularities of this environment, we performed an extensive range of tests and experiments to see which positions actually allow for pleasant ways of working and which parts of the body need support for comfortable leaning or reclining. The aim of the project was to afford positions that are only comfortable for 20 to 60 minutes, instead of the familiar postures that can be used throughout an entire work day. This temporary comfort of individual positions promotes exploration of the landscape of affordances offered by the installation as a whole. By inviting people to assume a variety of working positions, *The End of Sitting* made people aware of the way their bodies normally take certain environmental regularities for granted.

Specialists from the field of human movement sciences observed the behaviour of people who were asked to work in the installation and provide feedback on the design. The subjects of the first empirical study, conducted by Rob Withagen and Simone Caljouw,

reported that, compared to a traditional open-office setting, *The End of Sitting* was more pleasant to work in and better for their well-being.[15] The architectural concept of temporary comfort in a landscape of affordances for various positions clarifies why it was observed that 'many participants worked in several postures and changed location'.[16] The installation managed to motivate people to move more: only 17 per cent of participants worked in just one posture, demonstrating the dynamic of alternation of non-sitting postures we had in mind. The subjects also reported that while their legs were more tired after working in the standing office, they felt more energetic. Furthermore, the study suggests that productivity was on par with more conventional office settings.

The more recent project *Breaking Habits* (2017) follows up on *The End of Sitting* by exploring possibilities for an environment without chairs that might be applicable to a private setting. This experimental domestic landscape of the future that breaks with entrenched living habits is on display at the headquarters of the Mondriaan Fund for Visual Art in Amsterdam. Just like offices and other spaces of our sedentary society, most living rooms are furnished entirely around the possibility of sitting down. *Breaking Habits* explores what a world without chairs and sofas might look like. This art installation turns a philosophical worldview into a tangible, material reality: a diagonal landscape of affordances that provides a scaffold for a more active lifestyle by inviting users to change positions and explore new diagonal standing postures. Using more horizontal (but still diagonal) surfaces and applying a softer material, the affordances provided by this particular installation cater more to the relaxing environment of a dwelling but still omit the sofas and armchairs that have been a part of Western living rooms from time immemorial. Will diagonal living become the new norm?

Conclusion

Insights from ecological psychology have led RAAAF to an understanding of our built environment as part of a dynamic system of ecological niches that accommodates humans and their abilities and practices. The related notion of affordances – possibilities for action offered by the environment – allows us to treat architecture, art and the process of making as an integral element of this system. By using art installations to create new affordances and explore or reveal existing ones, we can offer new approaches for existing practices or even change them for the better.

PATCHWORK METROPOLIS

Regional Study by Willem Jan Neutelings

In 1989, the municipality of The Hague commissioned architect Willem Jan Neutelings (1959) to study the urbanization process of the southern section of the Randstad conurbation in the west of the Netherlands, with particular attention to its southern wing, the area between The Hague and Rotterdam.

Neutelings' proposal for a *tapijtmetropool,* or patchwork metropolis, rejects the traditional contrast between the city and the outlying rural areas, and replaces this binary opposition with a conception of the region as a networked collage of disparate fragments: traffic infrastructure, residential areas, historical inner cities, open areas, old estates, greenhouses, industry, leisure and so on. Neutelings argued that the modern urban landscape at the end of the twentieth century was no longer constituted by a practice of continuous urban expansion, where the 'red' cities eat away the 'green' that surrounds them on the map. He rejected this dichotomy and conceptualized the Randstad as a heterogeneous patchwork, where developments are constituted by the transformation of fragments within this patchwork.

Crucially, this patchwork was to be understood not just on the level of urbanization patterns, but also on the sociocultural level. The social fabric of the Randstad is understood as an amalgam of different and diverse subcultures and lifestyles that – just like the physical morphology of the carpet metropolis – is subject to constant change. As such, the city is no longer understood as belonging to a homogeneous and singular 'society' the way it had been during the days of welfare state planning.

Accordingly, Neutelings presented a varied landscape for different lifestyles on the southern edge of The Hague around the A4 motorway and the former Ypenburg airfield that accounts for a diverse typology of niche cultures: golf greens in the centre of the Hague, an urban square for big manifestations located under a motorway junction, a 'hill city' on top of former garbage dumps in Rijswijk and a set of high-rises known as 'Ypenburg City' superimposed on the motorway itself.

Heuvelstad (Hill City), 1989

Nietstad (Non-City), 1989

Plein 1999 (Square 1999,
below the Prins Clausplein),
1989

Golfstad (Golf City), 1989

Ypenburg City, 1989

Patchwork Metropolis in the
Rotterdam-The Hague region,
1990

Willem Jan Neutelings

1/15　　　　　　　　　　　　　　　　　　　　　　　　　　'GOLFSTAD' vuy '84

ワッセナー市役所

'Yperbug City' uy/89

1/15

THE NEW NETHERLANDS 2050

Scenarios for *Nederland Nu Als Ontwerp*
by Peter Terreehorst

In 1987 the exhibition 'Nieuw Nederland, onderwerp van ontwerp' (The new Netherlands, object of design) took place in H.P. Berlage's Amsterdam Stock Exchange. The exhibition was the initiative of the foundation Nederland Nu Als Ontwerp (The Netherlands Now As Design) with urban planner Dirk Frieling as chairman. With a view to the future urbanization of the Netherlands, four scenarios were developed for the spatial development of the Netherlands up to the year 2050 in order to elucidate the urgent choices for politicians and the public.

The four scenarios met different political visions of the future: 'careful', 'critical', 'dynamic' and 'relaxed'. The first three reflect the demographic and economic projections and wishes of the three main streams in Dutch politics at the time: respectively those of the confessional Christian Democratic Party, the Social Democrats, and the Liberals. The fourth, 'relaxed' scenario offers a problem-solving 'technocratic' approach, elaborated by the initiators of the event.

Among the many subprojects proposed for the various scenarios were the 'Eropolis', an offshore hotel containing as many as 700,000 rooms designed by Carel Weeber, and a scheme for the development of high-tech agro industry along with housing and recreational areas right next to Schiphol airport proposed by OMA. Architect Pi de Bruijn ended up not turning in his design for a 'health network' focused on eastern Noord-Brabant, because the bounds of the Christian 'careful' scenario did not allow his suggested inclusion of genetic manipulation, social planning and internationalization of the area.

For the 'relaxed' scenario, engineer Peter Terreehorst designed a new landscape in the southwestern province of Zeeland inspired by the monumental Delta Works that protect the Dutch delta landscape of former estuaries and islands from the natural impact of the North Sea. The plan by Terreehorst combines issues of food production and sea defences with provisions for tourism and dynamic landscape formation to meet seemingly opposite needs. In a series of steps from 1990 up to 2050, the plan proposes to work towards an assembly of 'fast breeding ponds' for fish and shellfish (so-called maricultures), recreational facilities and residential areas. Together, these steps would result in an ecosystem that would make the southwestern Dutch delta future-proof in all these aspects.

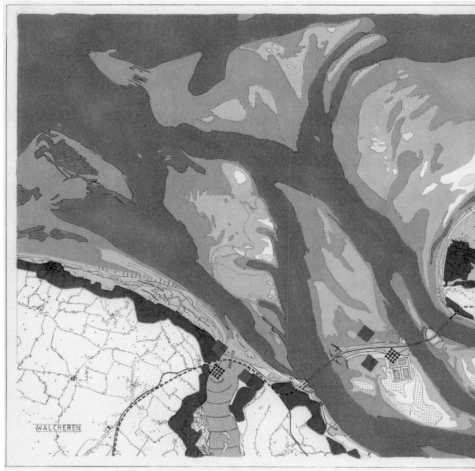

Future vision for coastal ponds along the Dutch coast, presented as part of the event *Nederland Nu Als Ontwerp*, 1987: phase 1, 1990; and phase 2, 2010

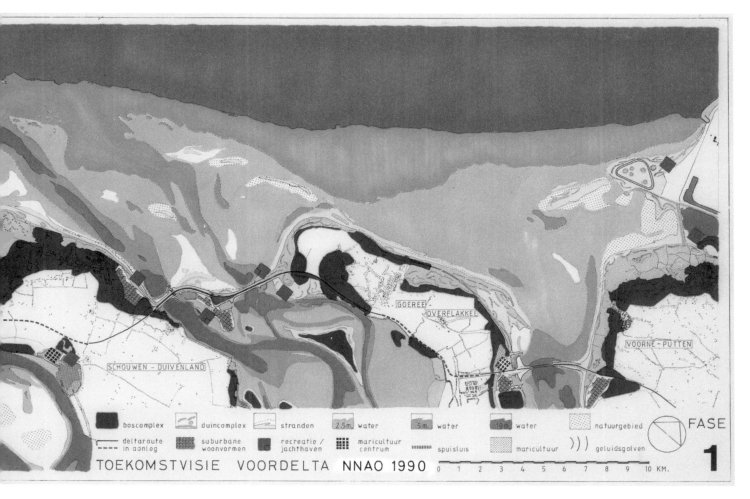

boscomplex — duincomplex — stranden — 2.5m. water — 5m. water — 10m. water — natuurgebied — deltaroute in aanleg — suburbane woonvormen — recreatie / jachthaven — maricultuur centrum — spuisluis — maricultuur — geluidsgolven — FASE

GOEREE - OVERFLAKKEE

VOORNE - PUTTEN

SCHOUWEN - DUIVENLAND

TOEKOMSTVISIE VOORDELTA NNAO 1990   0 1 2 3 4 5 6 7 8 9 10 KM.   **1**

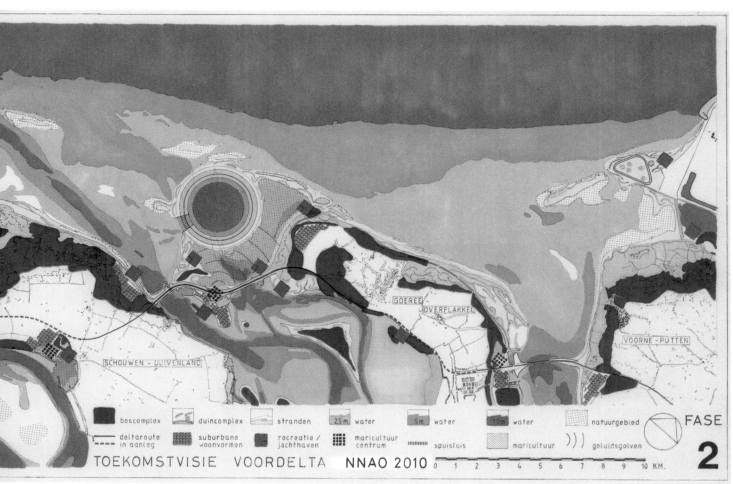

boscomplex — duincomplex — stranden — 2.5m. water — 5m. water — 10m. water — natuurgebied — deltaroute in aanleg — suburbane woonvormen — recreatie / jachthaven — maricultuur centrum — spuisluis — maricultuur — geluidsgolven — FASE

GOEREE - OVERFLAKKEE

VOORNE - PUTTEN

SCHOUWEN - DUIVENLAND

TOEKOMSTVISIE VOORDELTA NNAO 2010   0 1 2 3 4 5 6 7 8 9 10 KM.   **2**

Peter Terreehorst

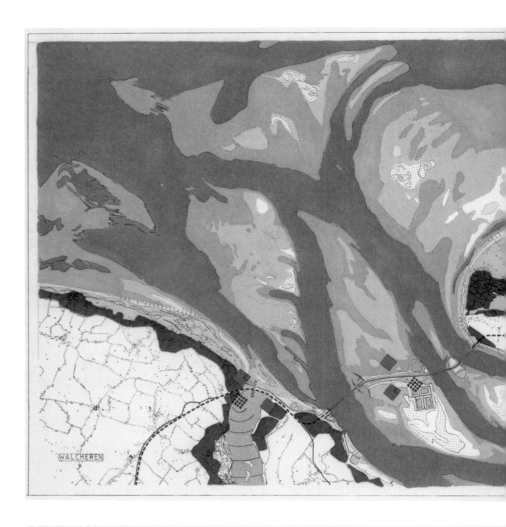

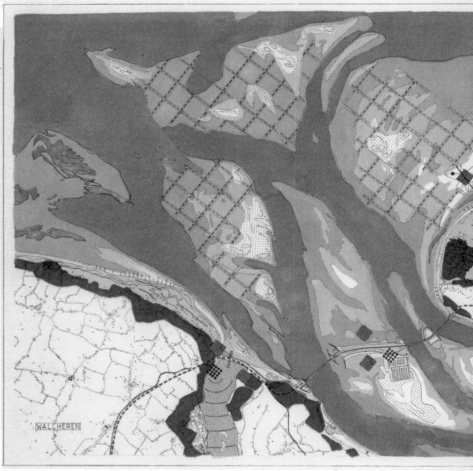

Future vision for coastal
ponds along the Dutch
coast, presented as part of
the event *Nederland Nu Als
Ontwerp*, 1987: phase 3,
2030; and phase 4, 2050

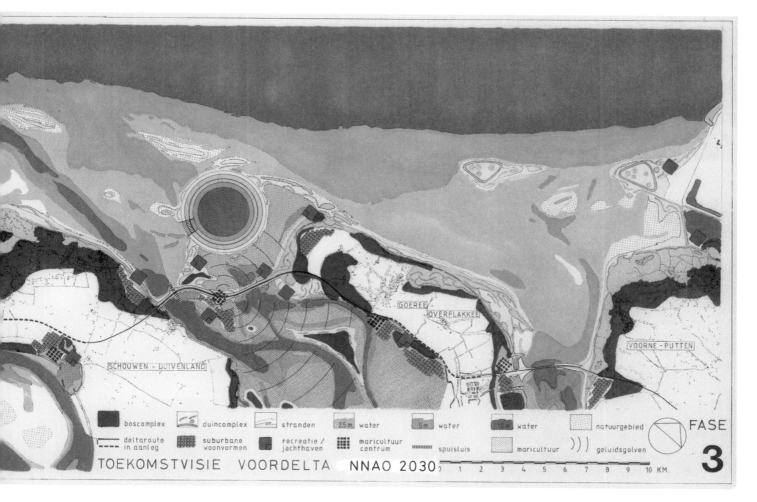

SCHOUWEN - DUIVENLAND

GOEREE OVERFLAKKEE

VOORNE - PUTTEN

FASE 3

TOEKOMSTVISIE VOORDELTA   NNAO 2030

0 1 2 3 4 5 6 7 8 9 10 KM.

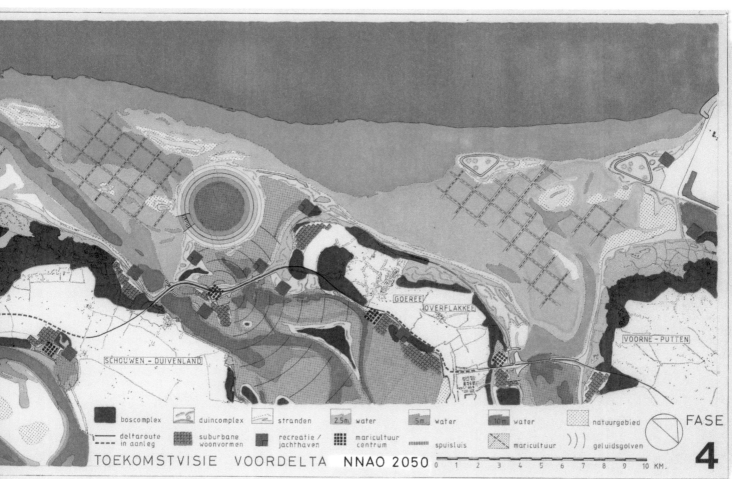

SCHOUWEN - DUIVENLAND

GOEREE OVERFLAKKEE

VOORNE - PUTTEN

FASE 4

TOEKOMSTVISIE VOORDELTA   NNAO 2050

0 1 2 3 4 5 6 7 8 9 10 KM.

Peter Terreehorst

Frits Palmboom

RETRACING HABITAT

Growth and Change in the Dutch Delta

Southwestern view of the Royal Crescent and surrounding landscape, Bath

Aerial photograph of the Nidda Valley with the colonies of Römerstadt and Praunheim

1   Like the ones found at the exhibition 'Habitat: Expanding Architecture', held in Het Nieuwe Instituut in 2018-2019, and elsewhere in this book.

2   Peter Smithson, *Bath, Walks within the Walls* (Bath: Adams & Dart, 1971).

3   Otto Das, Gerrit Oorthuys, Max Risselada, USSR 1917-1933 – Architectuur en Stedebouw, exhibition catalogue (Delft: TH Delft, 1969)

4   Hubert de Boer, Wouter Reh and Tjeerd Deelstra were teachers at the Architecture Faculty of TH Delft, and regularly published about landscape items in the journal *Wonen-TA/BK* (issues May 1971, April 1972, July 1972)

5   Aldo van Eyck, 'Kaleidoscope of the Mind', in: Rolf Sauer, James Bryan and Thomas Gilmore (eds.), *VIA 1: Ecology in Design* (Philadelphia: Graduate School of Fine Arts, University of Pennsylvania, 1968), 90-130.

6   Ruud Brouwers, 'De zaak Alphen', *Wonen-TA/BK* 38/16 (1973), 10-14.

7   Frits Palmboom, 'Werken vanuit "plek en proces" contra de balletjes vierkantjes en sterretjes', *Wonen-TA/BK* 38/16 (1973), 15-20.

In the 1960s and 1970s, urban design and architecture were dominated by large-scale housing production, new road construction and urban expansion. New residential and industrial areas mushroomed on freshly-created plains of sand around the cities. As a schoolboy I liked to go bike riding, either through the countryside or across the city. I was fascinated by the spectacle of construction and set out to absorb these new worlds. There was something compelling about their atmosphere of newness and optimism. While attending secondary school I started to read up on the subject and my decision to study architecture matured.

When I started in Delft in 1970, discussions flared about the downsides of the era of post-war reconstruction and prosperity growth: about standardization and monotony – the struggle with the 'aesthetics of the greater number' – about environmental pollution, the decay of the old cities and the impending obliteration of the countryside. Themes tabled in the 1950s and 1960s – in Dubrovnik among other places – were still being addressed by Team 10 members, with Aldo van Eyck, Herman Hertzberger and Jaap Bakema, among others, as spokespersons. They made sure that the elements that make up our 'habitat' were no longer primarily meant to be considered in terms of their *functional* significance, but mainly in terms of their *relational* value: their relationships to one another, through various scale levels and in interaction with their users. Dwellings were seen as 'parts of a community', whose arrangement was to allow 'growth and change' over time. All of this came with an architectural quest for new forms of spatiality that focused on 'in-between spaces' and 'reciprocity'.

These notions led to numerous designs for new arrangements of dwellings bearing names such as 'housing unit', 'visual group', 'isolate', 'village' or 'district'.[1] On the larger scale of urban and landscape design, however, they met with little response. This level remained the domain of planners, traffic engineers and urban designers for whom the doctrine of the separation of functions had become self-evident. Although the mechanical repetition of new housing districts in subsequent new rings around the city was indeed questioned, alternative models hung on to dreamy utopian vistas, including Constant Nieuwenhuys's New Babylon, or hardly subtle schemes for linear cities. New Babylon may well have been the symbol of the new, free living environment that was not looking for the cradle of a concentric district or neighbourhood but saw the entire territory of city and countryside as its playing field instead. Taking some liberty, Bakema's Pampus Plan can be seen as a cast-in-concrete derivative of this.

In the meantime, educators at the Faculty of Architecture in Delft – partly inspired by Peter and Alison Smithson – rediscovered Bath as a city nestling in and opening up to the countryside.[2] Twentieth-century equivalents such as the districts that the Frankfurt-based Ernst May gently arranged in the Niddadal landscape in the 1920s and 1930s were studied extensively. Max Risselada and Gerrit Oorthuys tracked down forgotten Constructivist plans for linear urbanization in the early Soviet Union and exhibited them in Delft.[3] In the wake of the teachings by Jan Bijhouwer from Wageningen, Hubert de Boer and Wouter Reh brought knowledge about the landscape as a phenomenon in itself.[4] Chris van Leeuwen, the grand old man of the young discipline of ecology, held well-attended lectures and study groups. All of this gave content and substance to the 'spirit of ecology in design', which van Eyck previously proclaimed was 'the only way to counteract erosion'.[5]

Together, they informed the search for a different, 'reciprocal' relationship between city and territory.

Alphen aan den Rijn

In 1973, against this background, young teachers Gerrit Smienk and Yap Hong Seng organized a design project for Alphen aan den Rijn, a small town in the middle of the Green Heart of the Dutch Randstad that, like many other towns, was experiencing a sudden boom. They were trying to find alternatives to the concentric expansions provided for in the then applicable zoning plan made by urban development agency Kuiper Compagnons. They foresaw that the tripling of its population would create an Alphen 'stuck between town and village', dependent on 'roads that will never be built', and would 'connect insufficiently with the qualities of the landscape'.[6]

The challenge of the project was to wrench the desire for a 'landscape-specific city' away from schematic or utopian ideal models and test it on the concrete topography of the actual countryside.

Involved in the project as a third-year student, I designed a proposal for a cautious process of incremental urbanization, building on the corridor of river, road and railway between Alphen and Leiden.[7]

Reading back, the extent to which this proposal centred on concepts such as 'growth' and 'change' is striking. The on-the-spot addition of dwellings to facilities and public transport lines already present would allow the creation of new cores or densifications that would in turn allow further growth. An important source of inspiration were ecological ideas that focused on the interweaving of 'pattern' and 'process' and in which the dimension of time played a crucial role.

**Frits Palmboom, reconstruction
of map of Rotterdam as drawn by
Pjotr Gonggrijp, c. 1980**

**Frits Palmboom, redrawn map
of Rotterdam, c. 1980**

8   Pjotr Gonggrijp, 'De straat en
het landschap', De Straat – vorm van
samenleven (Eindhoven: stedelijk
Van Abbemuseum, 1972), 78-82.

150

At the same time, the design was a search for a form language that would be able to articulate a relaxed relationship between city and countryside.

An important source of inspiration was Pjotr Gonggrijp's 1969 graduation work, which consisted of an investigation into the Dutch landscape by the redrawing of its map: not as a functional 'machine', with the accompanying emphasis on the infrastructure of railways, canals, traffic routes and administrative boundaries, but as a spatial phenomenon. He started with the flows of streams, creeks and rivers and the constellation of soil types in light pastel shades; a shower of dots represented buildings, yards and groups of trees; urban cores around streets and squares were precise miniatures in red; railway lines and motorways light pencil lines. An intriguing aspect is that he used maps from very different periods: Jacob van Deventer's city maps from the sixteenth century, the earliest topographical maps from around 1850 and contemporary road maps including the projections that according to the *Tweede Nota Ruimtelijke Ordening* (the second Dutch national policy memorandum on spatial planning) were planned for the end of the twentieth century. They exude a notion of *longue durée* that was largely lacking in the thinking of planners at the time.

Together all of those dots, stripes and strokes create a kind of galaxy that locally threads together to form lines or garlands – along the beach ridges, along river banks, river dikes and reclamation strips – and densify into crystalline hubs in the cities.

When he zooms in on Middelburg in Walcheren or Leiden at the beach ridges, he shifts from registration to interpretation: names spatial patterns, compositional principles and the connected spatial relationships between large and small, high and low, wet and dry, clear and diffuse: the 'twin phenomena' of Aldo van Eijck, detected in the flat and vast Dutch countryside.[8] I saw in them the promise of an 'animate' urbanism that would bring city and countryside together.

Thus inspired, I also started the project for Alphen aan den Rijn by redrawing the map, with similar perseverance and precision. It opened my eyes to the lines and ribbons, the constellations and local conglomerations along the railway line from Alphen to Leiden with transverse roads, waterways and lines of windmills running across the surrounding polder landscape like tentacles. In them I recognized potential starting points for an open and linear urbanization pattern.

Most of the new residential areas are schematically indicated as soft-red spots, with curved edges that embrace the open space like crescents.

At the same time, places where countryside and buildings meet in an almost architectural way (a three-forked road with old ruins, church tower, lines of windmills and wide view of the polder landscape) are worked out more meticulously. I would later start to refer to such elaborations as 'crucial details' that bring the large scale of urban planning to life on a smaller scale. Linear compositions intersected by occasional meandering creek ridges and more sculptural forms compete for priority. The inspirations from Bath and Frankfurt are – slightly unresolved – on the surface. But, with the benefit of hindsight, the tone appears to have been set.

Rotterdam, verstedelijkt landschap

As I was redrawing the map for Alphen aan den Rijn, I also came across traces of the episodes that Gonggrijp had left out of his maps: speculative urbanization of the nineteenth century, modernist districts on levelled ground, heavy infrastructure and traffic systems that took little notice of the countryside's subsurface. Later, in the context of my projects in Rotterdam, the question of the fragmentation of the contemporary urban landscape became increasingly pressing. Both my 1981 graduation project and my first job took place here. I incorporated my experiences and observations in my book *Rotterdam, verstedelijkt landschap* (1987).

During my graduation period, I compared the Rotterdam Gonggrijp represented on one of his many maps to my sketch of Rotterdam as I found it in the 1970s and 1980s.

The more recent image shows an entire new system: a large-scale grid of traffic lines. The compartments it encloses contain a seemingly random mix of subdivisions of different cuts and sizes: from the large rectangular arrangements of the modernist residential districts to the diffuse, semi-accidental and directionless layout of the 1970s districts (known in the Netherlands as 'cauliflower districts'). Urbanization seems to take place mainly by grid compartment, no longer linearly.

However, these compartments still show traces of the linear patterns detected by Gonggrijp – the long ribbons, river embankments, river dikes and so on – albeit often heavily deformed, cut and bent to size and changed in shape. Some of these long lines have retained their original continuity and run across several sections. Almost casually, they link up the different parts of the city and the landscape.

The two drawings represent the problem that was central to my study of Rotterdam as an urbanized landscape in a nutshell. How are the different systems related? Gradually my interest shifted from the directly

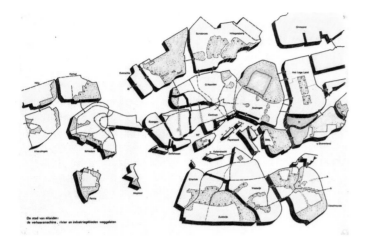

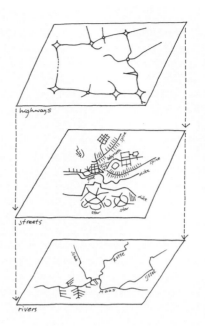

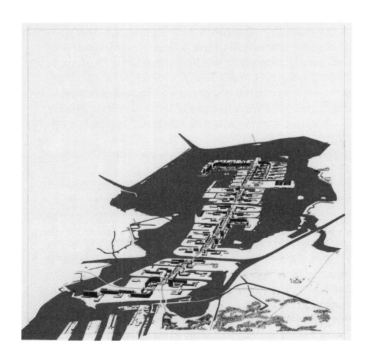

Frits Palmboom, drawing of the 'agglomeration of islands' that is left of Rotterdam once rivers, railroad tracks and motorways are omitted from the map, 1987

Frits Palmboom, drawing of three constitutive layers of Rotterdam: motorway frame, streets, rivers, 1987

Van den Broek and Bakema, perspective drawing of the Pampus extension plan, Amsterdam, 1964

Aerial photograph of IJburg, Amsterdam

9   Frits Palmboom, *Rotterdam Verstedelijkt Landschap* (Rotterdam: Uitgeverij 010, 1987), 65.
10   Design for IJburg, *Nota van Uitgangspunten* (City of Amsterdam, 1995).
11   Frits Palmboom, *IJsselmeergebied: Een ruimtelijk perspectief* (Nijmegen: Vantilt, 2018).

perceptible grouping of buildings and vegetation in space to the underlying systems on which they were grafted, as it were, such as parcellation, drainage, access and ownership structure. In the book I called these 'the system of plots, ditches and roads'.

Essentially, *Rotterdam, verstedelijkt landschap* was also based on the redrawing of the map. However, the emphasis was less on the objects – the galaxies of dots – and more on the lines as organizing principles.

The lines facilitate the flows in the city – of water, people, ships, cars, trains – and guide the experience of space *in motion*.

The lines originate from the historical process of landscape formation. In the course of time they change colour. Creeks become ribbons, ditches become streets, canals and rivers absorb railway tracks, railway lines become cycle paths and so on.

The different flows have their own dynamics and operation. This is how the idea of three constituent layers crystallized: the system of rivers and dikes of the delta, the system of plots, ditches, roads and city streets and the system of railways and motorways, the 'traffic machine', which connects over great distances, but at the same time divides the city into compartments.

Although these layers differ in origin and age, for designers they don't impose a predefined hierarchical relationship; they are of equal value, all three have their necessity and relevance. Their simultaneous presence colours the experience of the contemporary city: 'Numerous unexpected combinations and contrasts are the result.'[9] Urban design centres on shaping their mutual relations.

The aim of tracing and copying this jumble of lines and systems was to understand and identify the complex composition they hid. Drawing tricks did help: drawing things on top of each other or pulling them apart – simplifying, omitting, exaggerating, reversing, cutting out, hanging one over the other. It became more and more clear to me that copying the map equalled constructing a new image, which prepares the shift from analysis to design. Urban design mainly concerns the spatial organization of the ground, which precedes construction.

IJburg Amsterdam

With the Design for IJburg, we re-entered an arena: that in which Bakema drew his linear urban expansion of Amsterdam in 1964-1965. In principle, his Pampus Plan followed an unambiguous linear city scheme: a series of 'housing units' threaded together on a continuous transport axis across the IJmeer. He translated this scheme into a sculptural mega-architecture that curled around the island of Pampus, with residual sheets of water as a background.

The new design for IJburg did not primarily focus on the expressive form of the urban buildings, but on the shape of the expanse of water: on the design of the spaces between the islands, on which the urban expansion was to take place. It formed the spatial introduction to the almost unlimited openness of the IJmeer/Markermeer – part of the catchment area of the entire Dutch delta and therefore also part of a much larger ecological framework. The idea of the continuous strip of urbanization has been abandoned for the idea of an archipelago, in direct contact with the water of the entire inland sea.[10] Landscape architect Dirk Sijmons, who prepared the urban design assignment for IJburg certainly had a hand in this. He was one of the students who helped to bring Chris van Leeuwen to Delft at the time and he devoted his career to the anchoring of ecological thinking in spatial design.

'The water's in charge, the city's a guest' became its motto. The configuration of land and water has a rather erratic shape, influenced by water currents, wind directions, water depths, soil types, ecological relationships, shipping routes, high-voltage power lines and so on. It is actually a three-dimensional design for the ground, with shorelines varying per island and curving or moving to accommodate the open spaces of the expanse of water, with a number of striking corner points, strategically placed bridges, main access lines and only sparing suggestions – as 'crucial details' – for buildings in characteristic locations. The design for the ground is a spatial framework in which buildings can nestle in the course of time and thus allows 'growth and change'.

Each island has been provided with different characteristics: *systems* for access, drainage and subdivision, translated into *cross sections* with dikes, ground-level heights, water depths, vessel-related vertical clearance heights, and so on. They still distantly echo Joost Vahl's plans for Tanthof, which I followed with great interest in the 1970s. These, too, distanced themselves from the architectural mega-shape and searched for an 'organization of the ground'. But unlike in Tanthof, in IJburg the framework has a clearly designed form, with detailed transverse and linear profiles that give the framework its own scale and shape. This way the framework can mediate between the small and the large scale – even if it embodies a dimension of infinity.

During my recent occupation of the Van Eesteren Chair at Delft University of Technology, I have developed this even further.[11] Spread across the entire delta

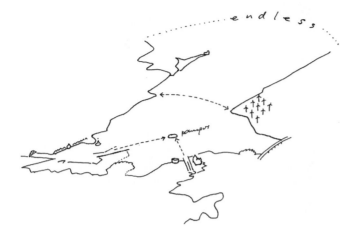

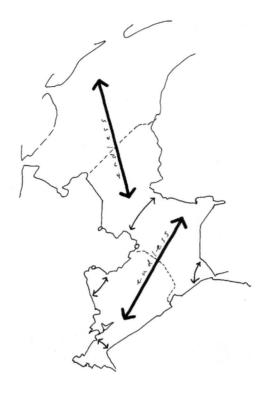

**Frits Palmboom, drawings
of the infinite nature of
the longitudinal axes of
the IJsselmeer, 2018**

12   As did the exhibition 'Habitat: Expanding Architecture', held in Het Nieuwe Instituut in Rotterdam in 2018-2019, curated by Dirk van den Heuvel, see: totalspace. hetnieuweinstituut.nl/en/ habitat-expanding-architecture.

13   It simultaneously relates to different social practices of cultivation of the land in the course of time.

14   Alison and Peter Smithson, *Urban Structuring* (London/New York: Studio Vista/Reinhold Publishing Corporation, 1967), 51.

15   Alison and Peter Smithson, from their Valley Section grid for the Dubrovnik conference, Fold Houses, panel 4, 1955-1956.

16   Compare the drawings and texts in Willem Jan Neutelings' *Tapijtmetropool*: they accurately describe the fragmented condition of the urbanized landscape – but leave out the 'stratification' of layers within and between the fragments (the resistance of time).

17   See also Frits Palmboom, 'Drawing the Ground, Layering Time', introductory essay in: *Drawing the Ground – Landscape Urbanism Today: The work of Palmbout Urban Landscapes* (Basel: Birkhauser Verlag, 2010).

landscape, settlements form links between land and water, between areas inside and outside the dikes, between 'place' and 'space'. Of this, IJburg is a contemporary version. On the large scale of the entire IJsselmeer region we drew and identified a number of compositional principles that supported the experience of openness and infinity that is strongly felt by every inhabitant and visitor: the longitudinal axes of the inland sea, which link the only just visible delta landscape to the North Sea and the ocean.

Valley Section and Layer Approach

It is interesting to look back on this work in the larger context of the discipline.[12] Through drawings and texts a partly 'posthumous dialogue' between generations unfolds. In retrospect, this makes fragments visible of a prior history of which I was only partially aware at the time.

Strikingly, Patrick Geddes's Valley Section played quite a prominent role in the conception of the notion 'habitat' at the time of the 1956 CIAM conference in Dubrovnik. A *cross section* of the countryside – not a map – is taken as a reference for the discussion on settlement forms. From ridge to ridge, the Valley is a directly perceptible, three-dimensional entity that is spatially comprehensible and lends itself to an 'architectural' approach.[13]

This resonates the strongest in the examples and designs presented by Alison and Peter Smithson. In modernist urban design the ground was usually seen as a clean slate, a neutral plane for the projection of a future ideal, preferably in the service of all – hence, free of interests, property claims and history. The Smithsons were perhaps the first to address the *physical form of the ground* as a design theme. Not only at the level of the building or a group of buildings, but up to the level of entire cities or agglomerations: 'Traditionally, some unchanging large-scale feature – the Acropolis, the River, the Canal, or some unique configuration of the ground – was the thing that made the whole community structure comprehensible and assured the identity of the parts within the whole.'[14]

Their designs show a search for an intimate, material connection of the habitat and the basic form of the landscape. It evoked the promise of site-specific architecture and a new perspective on time and history, 'like new fruit on old twigs'.[15] Their contribution has a strong atmospheric quality (material, tactile, with patina), which extends far beyond the canonical imagery of modernism. To this day, I experience them as an inexhaustible source of inspiration.

In retrospect, the panels that Romke de Vries presented in Dubrovnik in 1956 are the strongest Dutch equivalent. He shows how his designs for different types of housing units nestle in the actual landscape of the Low Countries. He illustrates this with images of waving reeds, wind-eroded dunes, water blown about – images that can measure up to those of Alison and Peter Smithson with their atmospheric qualities. They are stuck to a cross section of the whole of the Netherlands, in which the minimal relief of the flat land has been exaggerated: a Valley Section of the Low Land.

Another eye-opener was seeing Pjotr Gonggrijp's work against this background. He, too, transposes the three-dimensional Valley Section's way of looking and thinking to the extremely flat, two-dimensional countryside of the Dutch delta. In doing so, the scale shifts from a separately perceptible valley to the complete river basins of the Scheldt, Meuse, Waal and Rhine. He also shifts from a diagrammatic cross section à la Romke de Vries to the actual map. The map shows an enormous variety and wealth of settlement patterns per area. The city and countryside are not always in an immediately recognizable mutual relationship with each other. Sometimes it is clear, but often quite diffuse. This in itself is a constructive fact you can play with in a design. It later helped me to get a grip on the complexity of a city like Rotterdam and to look beyond the simple urban-rural dichotomy.

City and countryside overlap and mix, they pervade each other in thousands of variations and fall apart into disparate fragments: a complexity to which the notion of 'twin phenomenon' no longer seems to do justice.[16]

In my own work, I have increasingly related the spatial form of the 'habitat' to underlying systems and their associated dynamics.[17] Valley Section and layer approach have to do the work together. Beyond map images and actual cross sections, I look for the conceptual stratification in which time and history do their work – and, at the same time, for the sensory experience of 'place' and 'space'.

URBANIZED LANDSCAPES

Analyses and Designs by Frits Palmboom

As a student at Delft University of Technology, urban designer Frits Palmboom (1951) was inspired by the work and lectures of Pjotr Gonggrijp. His analytical maps showed Palmboom how drawing could be a way of reading the landscape, and understand the reciprocities between its material manifestation and its transformation through the impact of human inhabitation and intervention.

In 1973, Palmboom made an analysis of and design for the urbanization of the area around Alphen aan den Rijn, a small city situated in the peat pastures between Amsterdam, Rotterdam, The Hague and Utrecht. The influence of Gonggrijp on this study is clearly visible: based on a meticulous morphological analysis, Palmboom developed a linear urbanization model along a public transport line based on cycles of growth and change. His proposal was not a blueprint design to fixate a future condition, but a process-based scenario for urban development.

Fourteen years later, in 1987, Palmboom made his name with the book *Rotterdam, verstedelijkt landschap* (Rotterdam, urbanized landscape), which provided a completely new interpretation of the urban morphology of Rotterdam. Based on a historical analysis of the physical history of the urban landscape, Palmboom showed how a combination of the delta's geology, polder patterns and the damage of wartime bombardments in combination with the modernizing impulse of large-scale traffic and ports had led to the characteristic fragmented urban fabric – the urbanized landscape – of Rotterdam. His research for these analyses again shows how drawing different layers (infrastructural, morphological, historical, geographical) served as a way of reading the physical manifestation of the landscape, and its material coherence.

Together with Jaap van den Bout, Palmboom was involved in the design of IJburg (1995-1997), a large, new urban expansion realized on reclaimed land to the east of Amsterdam. Working in a team with H+N+S landscape architects and the City of Amsterdam, Palmboom and Van den Bout proposed an archipelago of islands. The project was aimed at achieving a new and balanced relationship between the large-scale, man-made landscape of the polders and the IJsselmeer area, and the physical morphology of the new extension. A vocabulary of transitions between water and land was developed with an eye for the experience of the vast water landscape.

Possible urban expansions
along the Rhine between
Leiden and Alphen aan den
Rijn, 1973

Proposal for urban expansion
of Koudekerk aan den Rijn,
1973

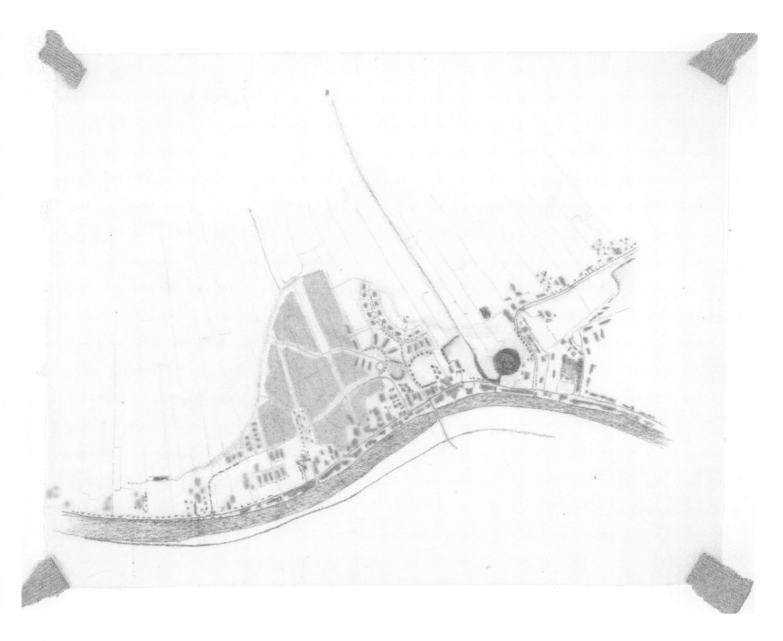

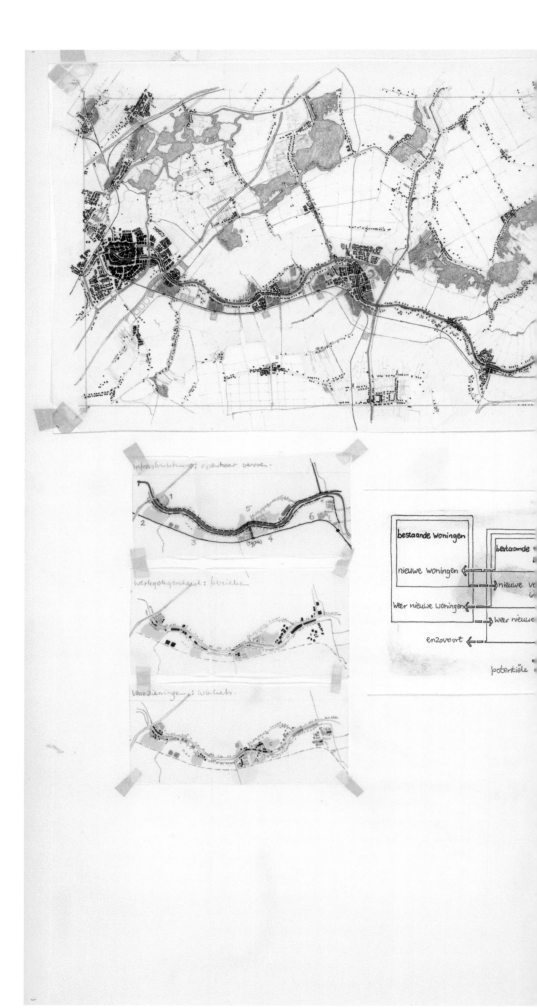

Collage of different forms of
urbanization between Leiden
and Alphen aan den Rijn
with photos of the existing
landscape, 1973

Frits Palmboom

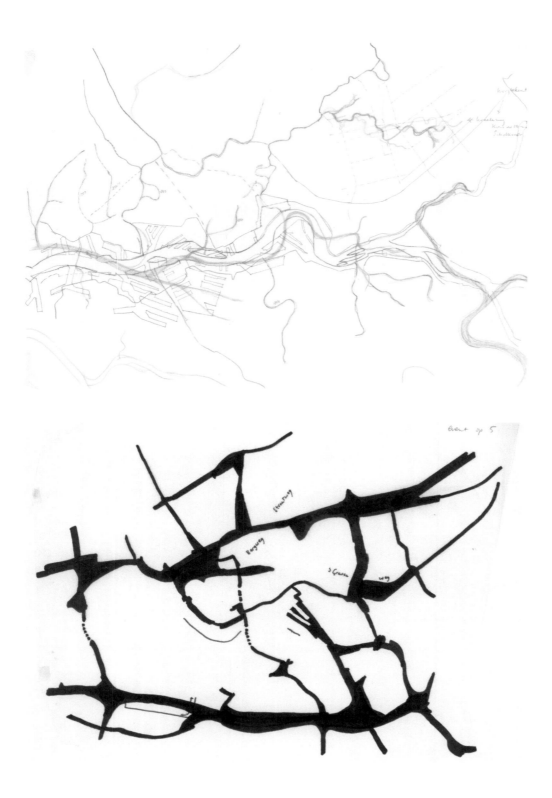

Diachronic study of
Rotterdam's river, waterways,
creeks and harbours, 1985

Study of Rotterdam's traffic
infrastructure, 1985

Study of Rotterdam's different
waterways, street patterns and
allotment structure, 1985

Study of Rotterdam's
morphological patterns, 1985

Urbanized Landscapes

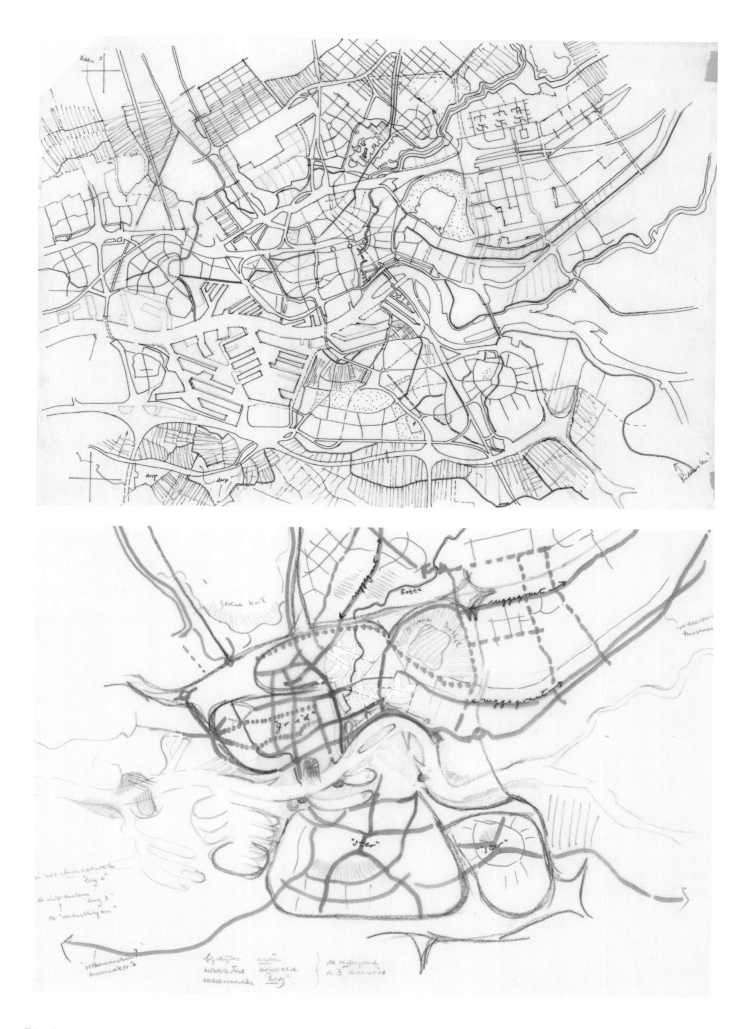

Frits Palmboom

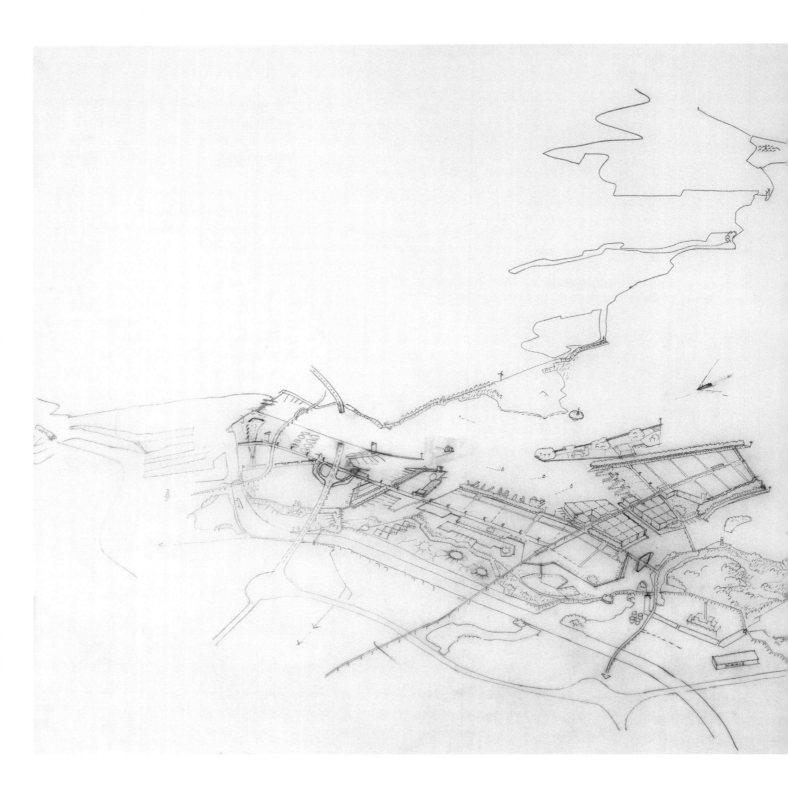

Bird's eye view of the design
for IJburg, 1995

Section of the islands,
IJburg, Amsterdam.
Drawing by Yttje Feddes, 1995

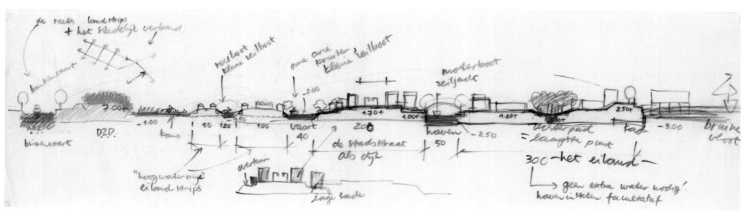

Frits Palmboom

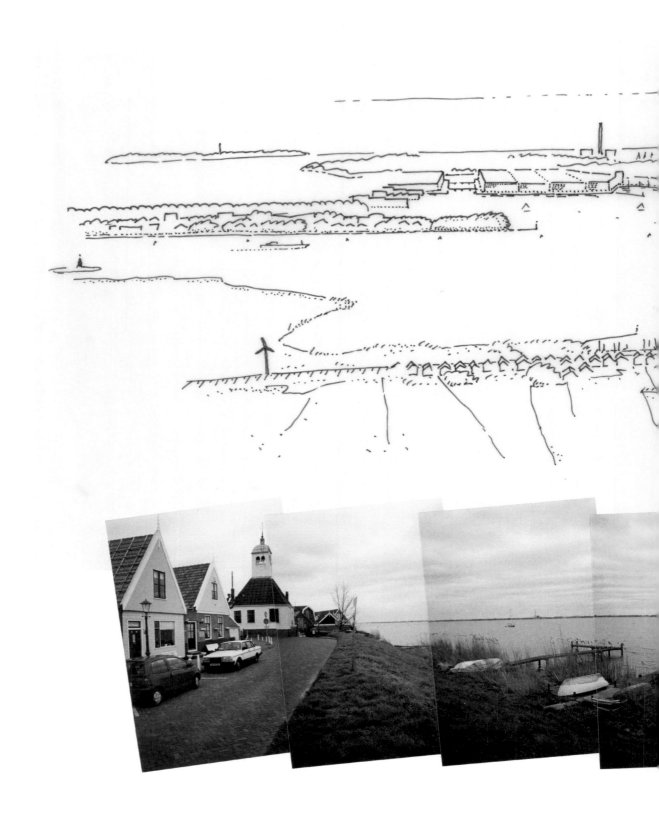

**Future silhouette of IJburg
as seen from Durgerdam, 1995**

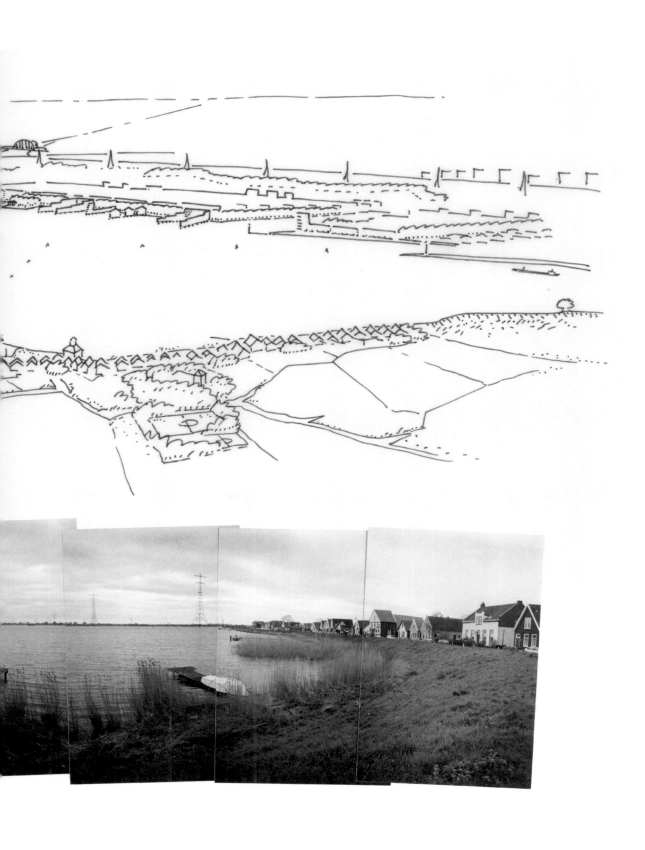

INDEX

BIOGRAPHIES

Dirk van den Heuvel is an associate professor at Delft University of Technology, and co-founder and head of the Jaap Bakema Study Centre at Het Nieuwe Instituut in Rotterdam. Van den Heuvel received a Richard Rogers Fellowship from Harvard University in 2017, and was a Visiting Scholar at Monash University in 2019. He was curator of the Dutch national pavilion for the Venice Architecture Biennale in 2014. Other exhibitions include 'Changing Ideals. Rethinking the House' (Bureau Europa, 2008), 'Structuralism' (HNI 2014, with H. Hertzberger), and 'Art on Display 1949-69' (Calouste Gulbenkian Museum 2019, with P. Curtis). Publications include *Jaap Bakema and the Open Society* (2018), *Architecture and the Welfare State* (2015, with M. Swenarton and T. Avermaete), *Team 10: In Search of a Utopia of the Present 1953-1981* (2005, with M. Risselada), *Alison and Peter Smithson: From the House of the Future to a House of Today (*2004, with M. Risselada). He is an editor of the publication series *DASH: Delft Architectural Studies on Housing* and the online journal for architecture theory *Footprint*. He also served on the board of *OASE journal for architecture*.

Janno Martens studied philosophy and architecture history at the University of Amsterdam. He is currently a doctoral candidate at KU Leuven, focusing on the intellectual history of architectural space between 1965 and 1980. He worked as research assistant for professor Erik Rietveld (UvA/ University of Twente) and as coordinator of the Jaap Bakema Study Centre. Recent publications include 'Sociomateriality and architecture: A Dutch tradition from Structuralism up to RAAAF' in *ONTO* (2019) and 'Two Birds: on Aldo van Eyck and Carel Visser' (coauthored with Laurens Otto) in *Orphanage Amsterdam: Building and Playgrounds by Aldo van Eyck* (2018). Other publications have appeared in academic periodicals such as *Phenomenology and the Cognitive Sciences* as well as on platforms for art and architecture including *De Witte Raaf, ArchiNed* and *Failed Architecture*.

Víctor Muñoz Sanz is an architect and researcher whose work examines architecture at the intersection of technology and management systems. He holds a degree in Architecture and a PhD cum laude from ETSA Madrid, and a Master's of Architecture in Urban Design from Harvard University. Muñoz Sanz was Harvard's Druker Fellow; emerging curator at the Canadian Centre for Architecture; coordinator of the Jaap Bakema Study Centre; co-principal researcher of 'Automated Landscapes' at Het Nieuwe Instituut; fellow at the Akademie Schloss Solitude; and is currently a researcher at Delft University of Technology. He has published essays in *Harvard Design Magazine, Bartlebooth, Work Body Leisure* (Hatje Cantz), *e-flux Architecture, Volume, Domus,* and *On Site Review.* His research on automation with Het Nieuwe Instituut was exhibited at the Venice Biennale.

Frits Palmboom studied urban planning at Delft University of Technology (TU Delft). From 1981, he worked for the Department of Urban Development of the City of Rotterdam. He founded his own office in 1990, and in 1994 he formed a partnership with Jaap van den Bout to become Palmboom & Van den Bout, which later became known as Palmbout Urban Landscapes. With this office, he was responsible for the design of IJburg, an urban extension consisting of artificial islands east of Amsterdam. Palmboom supervised the development of several Dutch areas, including Maastricht Belvedere and Zaanstad. In 2001, he was a guest professor of urban design at the KU Leuven, and from 2013 to 2016 he held the Van Eesteren Chair at the TU Delft. His publications include *Rotterdam, verstedelijkt landschap* (1987) and *IJsselmeer, a Spatial Perspective (*2018).

Erik Rietveld is Socrates professor at the University of Twente and a senior researcher at the University of Amsterdam. Earlier he was a fellow in Philosophy at Harvard University and a visiting scholar at UC Berkeley's Helen Wills Neuroscience Institute. Together with his brother Ronald Rietveld he founded the multidisciplinary studio for visual art, architecture and philosophy RAAAF (Rietveld Architecture-Art-Affordances). They were responsible for Vacant NL, the Dutch contribution to the Venice Architecture Biennale 2010. RAAAF was elected Dutch Architect of the Year 2013 and awarded the European Prize of Architecture 2017. Ronald and Erik Rietveld are members of The Society of Arts of The Royal Netherlands Academy of Arts and Sciences (KNAW). Erik Rietveld publishes frequently in international journals such as *Mind, Synthese, Trends in Cognitive Science (TiCS), BBS and Harvard Design Magazine.* His philosophical work on skilled action and affordances was awarded with a Rubicon-, VENI- and VIDI grant by the Netherlands Organization for Scientific Research (NWO), and with an ERC Starting Grant by the European Research Council.

Hadas A. Steiner is an associate professor at the University at Buffalo, SUNY, who researches cross-pollinations of technological, scientific and cultural aspects of architectural fabrication. She is currently working on a manuscript, *The Accidental Visitant,* which studies the impact of the modern field of ornithology on architecture and the conceptualization of the built environment as an ecosystem. Steiner is the author of *Beyond Archigram: The Technology of Circulation* (Routledge) and her scholarship and reviews have been published in *OCTOBER, Grey Room, New Geographies, Journal of the Society of Architectural Historians, Journal of Architectural Education, Journal of Architecture and arq.*

Georg Vrachliotis is professor of Architecture Theory and director of the architecture research archive at the Karlsruhe Institute of Technology (KIT). He was appointed Dean of the Faculty of Architecture 2016-2019. He is curator and (co) author of *Complexity: Design Strategy and World View* (with A. Gleiniger 2008), *Simulation: Presentation Technique and Cognitive Method* (with Andrea Gleiniger 2009), *Geregelte Verhältnisse: Architektur und technisches Denken in der Epoche der Kybernetik* (2009), *Structuralism Reloaded: Rule-Based Design in Architecture and Urbanism* (with T. Valena and T. Avermaete 2011), *Fritz Haller: Architect and Researcher* (with Laurent Stalder, 2014) and of *Frei Otto: Thinking by Modeling* (2017). Georg Vrachliotis is a member of the advisory board of the magazine *ARCH+.*

Leonardo Zuccaro Marchi graduated from A.S.P. Alta Scuola Politecnica, Politecnico di Milano and Politecnico di Torino. He obtained his PhD at IUAV and Delft University of Technology (TU Delft), as a Joint Doctorate. He was a post-doctoral fellow at KTH University in Stockholm. He taught at the TU Delft, the Politecnico di Milano and the UDEM-Universidad de Monterrey. He is currently a guest researcher at the TU Delft. He is the author of *The Heart of the City: Legacy and Complexity of a Modern Design Idea* (Routledge). He was runner-up of Europan 11 and winner, together with the Collective of Projects in Equipoise (Co-P-E), of Europan 14 in 2017 with the project 'The Productive Heart of Neu Ulm'.

Habitat and Architecture
Page 8 (left): Van Eesteren Archive, Het Nieuwe Instituut, Rotterdam
Page 8 (right): Team 10 Archive, Het Nieuwe Instituut, Rotterdam
Page 12 (top): Courtesy of Max Risselada
Page 12 (bottom): Team 10 Archive, Het Nieuwe Instituut, Rotterdam
Page 14 (left): Team 10 Archive, Het Nieuwe Instituut, Rotterdam
Page 14 (right): Team 10 Archive, Het Nieuwe Instituut, Rotterdam
Page 16: Van den Broek and Bakema Archive, Het Nieuwe Instituut, Rotterdam
Page 19 (top left): Photo by Wim Brisse / Aldo van Eyck Archive, Loenen
Page 19 (bottom left): Courtesy of RAAAF
Page 19 (right): J.B. Bakema Archive, Het Nieuwe Instituut, Rotterdam
Page 21: Team 10 Archive, Het Nieuwe Instituut, Rotterdam

Between Habiter and Habitat
Page 26: L'Architecture d'Aujourd'hui, 42-43 (1952): XV
Page 28 (left): © Fondation Le Corbusier, c/o Pictoright Amsterdam 2020
Page 28 (right): gta Archive, ETH Zurich
Page 30 (top left): Forbat Archive, ArkDes Archive, Stockholm
Page 30 (bottom left): Team 10 Archive, Het Nieuwe Instituut, Rotterdam
Page 30 (right): gta Archive, ETH Zurich
Page 32 (left): gta Archive, ETH Zurich
Page 32 (right): © Fondation Le Corbusier, c/o Pictoright Amsterdam 2020

From Microchips to Total Cities
Page 32: Fritz Haller Archive, gta Archive, ETH Zurich
Page 84 (top left): Fritz Haller Archive, gta Archive, ETH Zurich
Page 84 (bottom left): Photo by Christian Moser / Fritz Haller Archive, gta Archive, ETH Zurich
Page 84 (top right): Fritz Haller Archive, gta Archive, ETH Zurich
Page 84 (bottom right): Photo by Christian Moser / Fritz Haller Archive, gta Archive, ETH Zurich
Page 86 (top left): Photo by Robert Häusser / Courtesy Frei Otto Works Archive, saai – Southwest German Archives for Architecture and Civil Engineering, Karlsruhe Institute of Technology
Page 86 (bottom left): Fritz Haller Archive, gta Archive, ETH Zurich
Page 86 (right): Fritz Haller Archive, gta Archive, ETH Zurich
Pages 88, 89: All images Fritz Haller Archive, gta Archive, ETH Zurich

A Habitat Waiting to Be
Page 90 (left): Photo by Sam Lambert / Cedric Price Fonds, Canadian Centre for Architecture
Page 90 (right): Photo by William Gill / Wikimedia Commons
Page 92 (left): © Hulton-Deutsch Collection/CORBIS/Corbis via Getty Images
Page 92 (top right): Cedric Price Fonds, Canadian Centre for Architecture
Page 92 (bottom right): Courtesy of Zoological Society of London
Page 94: All images Cedric Price Fonds, Canadian Centre for Architecture
Page 96 (top left): Photo by Sam Lambert / Cedric Price Fonds, Canadian Centre for Architecture
Page 96 (bottom left): Photo by Sam Lambert / Cedric Price Fonds, Canadian Centre for Architecture
Page 96 (right): Photo by Central Press Photos, Ltd. /Cedric Price Fonds, Canadian Centre for Architecture

Architecture and Ecological Psychology
Page 128: Courtesy of RAAAF
Pages 132, 133: Courtesy of RAAAF
Page 130 (top left): Photo by Ricky Rijkemberg / Courtesy of RAAAF
Page 130 (bottom left): Photo by Jan Kempenaers / Courtesy of RAAAF
Page 130 (right): Courtesy of RAAAF
Page 134: Photo by Johannes Schwarz / Courtesy of RAAAF

Retracing Habitat
Page 148 (left): Walter Ison, The Georgian Buildings of Bath from 1700 to 1830 (Bath: Kingsmead Reprints, 1969)
Page 148 (right): Das neue Frankfurt: internationale Monatsschrift für die Probleme kultureller Neugestaltung, 4:1930, 84 / Institut für Stadtgeschichte, Stadt Frankfurt am Main
Page 150: All images personal Archive of Frits Palmboom
Page 152 (top left): Personal Archive of Frits Palmboom
Page 152 (bottom left): J.B. Bakema Archive, Het Nieuwe Instituut, Rotterdam
Page 152 (top right): Personal Archive of Frits Palmboom
Page 152 (bottom right): Photo by Marco van Middelkoop / Aerophoto-Schiphol
Page 154: All images personal Archive of Frits Palmboom

Habitat 1956
Dubrovnik Scroll by Alison and Peter Smithson
J.B. Bakema Archive, Het Nieuwe Instituut, Rotterdam

Social Spaces
CIAM 10 – Micro-scale
GAI (Group for Architectural Investigation): J.B. Bakema Archive, Het Nieuwe Instituut, Rotterdam.
CIAM-Austria: Collection University for Applied Arts Vienna
Aldo van Eyck: Aldo van Eyck archive, Loenen
MARS Group (Bill and Gillian Howell, John Killick, John Partridge): J.B. Bakema Archive, Het Nieuwe Instituut, Rotterdam
MARS Group (Alison and Peter Smithson): Smithson Family Collection
MARS Group (John Voelcker): J.B. Bakema Archive, Het Nieuwe Instituut, Rotterdam
MARS Group (James Stirling): James Stirling/Michael Wilford fonds, Canadian Centre for Architecture

Landscape Interventions
CIAM 10 – Meso-scale
CIAM Porto: Centro de Documentação, Facultade de Arquitectura, Universidade de Porto
MARS Group (Alison and Peter Smithson): Smithson Family Collection
PAGON (Progressive Architects Group Oslo Norway): J.B. Bakema Archive, Het Nieuwe Instituut, Rotterdam
CIAM Holland, Opbouw Group Rotterdam (R. Romke de Vries): J.B. Bakema Archive, Het Nieuwe Instituut, Rotterdam

Totalities
CIAM 10 – Macro-scale
CIAM Holland, Opbouw Group Rotterdam (Arnold Oyevaar and Hein Stolle): J.B. Bakema Archive, Het Nieuwe Instituut, Rotterdam
IAM Holland, Opbouw Group Rotterdam (Jaap Bakema and Jan Stokla): J.B. Bakema Archive, Het Nieuwe Instituut, Rotterdam
de 8 Amsterdam (Aldo van Eyck): Aldo van Eyck archive, Loenen
PTAH (Progrès, Téchnique, Architecture Helsinki): Museum of Finnish Architecture /J.B. Bakema Archive, Het Nieuwe Instituut, Rotterdam

Psycho-analysis of the Delta Landscape
All images: Pjotr Gonggrijp Archive, Het Nieuwe Instituut, Rotterdam

Tanthof Delft
Page 116, 118: All images Van den Broek and Bakema Archive, Het Nieuwe Instituut, Rotterdam (long-term loan from Broekbakema Architects)
Page 119: All images Joost Váhl Archive, Het Nieuwe Instituut, Rotterdam
Page 120, 121: Van den Broek and Bakema Archive, Het Nieuwe Instituut, Rotterdam
Page 122, 123: All images Van den Broek and Bakema Archive, Het Nieuwe Instituut, Rotterdam (long-term loan from Broekbakema Architects)
Page 124, 125 (top): J. B. Bakema Archive, Het Nieuwe Instituut, Rotterdam
Page 125 (bottom left): Joost Váhl Archive, Het Nieuwe Instituut, Rotterdam
Page 125 (bottom right): Van den Broek and Bakema Archive, Het Nieuwe Instituut, Rotterdam (long-term loan from Broekbakema Architects)
Page 126, 127 (top): Joost Váhl Archive, Het Nieuwe Instituut, Rotterdam
Page 127 (bottom right and left): Courtesy of Broekbakema Architects

Patchwork Metropolis
All images: Willem Jan Neutelings Archive, Het Nieuwe Instituut, Rotterdam

The New Netherlands
All images: Nederland Nu als Ontwerp Archive, Het Nieuwe Instituut, Rotterdam

Urbanized Landscapes
All images: Private archive of Frits Palmboom

This volume is published by the Jaap Bakema Study Centre/Het Nieuwe Instituut and nai010 Publishers. It is the outcome of the project 'Habitat: Expanding Architecture', which involved an exhibition organized and presented at Het Nieuwe Instituut from 19 October 2017 to 10 March 2018, in combination with research seminars, archive conversations and public lectures. A documentation of these events is available online: totalspace.hetnieuweinstituut.nl/en/habitat-expanding-architecture

Through its activities, Het Nieuwe Instituut aims to increase the appreciation of the cultural and social significance of architecture, design and digital culture and to strengthen the interaction among these disciplines. In a period characterized by radical change, Het Nieuwe Instituut wants to moderate, stimulate and facilitate debate about architecture, design and digital culture through research and a public programme. The broadening and deepening of the public's appreciation is a fundamental starting point. Het Nieuwe Instituut derives its special position to a significant degree from the range and unique importance of the National Collection for Dutch Architecture and Urban Planning, which it manages. The collection, which is growing constantly, has a central place in the institute's research and exhibitions programmes.

The Jaap Bakema Study Centre started life in 2013 as a collaboration between Het Nieuwe Instituut and Delft University of Technology's Faculty of Architecture and the Built Environment. Its aim is to instigate academic research, together with third parties, in the fields of architecture and urban design, and to communicate its development and results through a programme of public presentations. The holdings of the National Collection for Dutch Architecture and Urban Planning, which are kept at Het Nieuwe Instituut, form the basis for formulating a research programme that is situated at the intersection of advanced historical-theoretical studies and urgent social issues.

With thanks to
ArkDes Archive Stockholm, Tamara Bjazic Klarin, Broekbakema Architects, Canadian Centre for Architecture, Documentation Centre of the Faculty of Architecture at the University of Porto, Aldo van Eyck Archive, Pjotr Gonggrijp, gta Archives ETH Zürich, Heidelberg University Library, Institut für Stadtgeschichte Frankfurt, Nelson Mota, Eric Mumford, Foundation Le Corbusier, Frits Palmboom, RAAAF (Ronald and Erik Rietveld), saai – Southwest German Archives for Architecture and Civil Engineering, Karlsruhe Institute of Technology, Sammlung Universität für angewandte Kunst Wien, Smithson Family Archive, Zoological Society of London.

Additional research
Soscha Monteiro de Jesus

Jaap Bakema Study Centre scientific advisory board
Tom Avermaete (ETH Zürich)
Hetty Berens (HNI)
Maristella Casciato (Getty Institute)
Carola Hein (TU Delft)
Laurent Stalder (ETH Zürich)

Habitat: Expanding Architecture Exhibition credits

Curator
Dirk van den Heuvel
(Jaap Bakema Study Centre)

Research
Dirk van den Heuvel
Janno Martens
Víctor Muñoz Sanz
Ellen Smit

Spatial design
Eric Roelen

Graphic design
Christine Albers

Project management
Arianne van der Veen

Production
Malou Zumbrink

Conservation
Elza van den Berg
Jacoline Bodewes
Elsemiek Hofman

Translation
Jack Eden

Lenders
Frits Palmboom
Broekbakema

Consulted archives of Het Nieuwe Instituut
Archive Alison and Peter Smithson, Archive Team 10
Archive Cornelis van Eesteren (long-term loan from Van Eesteren-Fluck en Van Lohuizen Stichting)
Archive Joost Váhl
Archive Neutelings Riedijk Architecten
Archive Pjotr Gonggrijp (long-term loan from Pjotr Gonggrijp)
Archive Stichting Nederland Nu Als Ontwerp
Archive Van den Broek en Bakema (long-term loan from Broekbakema)

Research and archive seminars
1 November 2018,
    Leonardo Zuccaro Marchi
3 February 2019,
    Tanthof Working Group with Frans Hooykaas, Peter Lüthi, Joost Váhl, Hiwe Groenewolt and Anneloes Groenewolt-van den Berg
24 February 2019,
    Pjotr Gonggrijp and Frits Palmboom

Lectures
18 October 2018,
    Erik Rietveld,
    Affordances and Architecture
25 October 2018,
    Alessandra Ponte,
    Matters of Extraction
13 December 2018,
    Hadas Steiner, Birds of a Feather: From Habitus to Habitat
7 March 2019,
    Georg Vrachliotis,
    Open Systems and Total Cities

With thanks to
Catherine Blain, Pjotr Gonggrijp, Marcela Hanáčková, Nelson Mota, Frits Palmboom, Eeva Liisa Pelkonen, Monika Platzer, Gennaro Postiglione, Max Risselada, Ivan Rupnik, Renata Margaretic Urlic, Aldo van Eyck archive, Archivio Piero Bottoni, Dastu, Politecnico di Milano, Canadian Centre for Architecture, Documentation Centre of the Faculty of Architecture, Universidade de Porto, Sammlung Architekturzentrum Wien, Sammlung Universität für angewandte Kunst Wien, Smithson Family Archive.

Colophon

Editors
Dirk van den Heuvel, Janno Martens,
Víctor Muñoz Sanz

Texts
Guus Beumer, Dirk van den Heuvel,
Janno Martens, Erik Rietveld,
Frits Palmboom, Hadas A. Steiner,
Georg Vrachliotis, Leonardo Zuccaro
Marchi

Copy editing
InOtherWords, D'Laine Camp

Translation
InOtherWords, D'Laine Camp and
Maria van Tol (Palmboom)

Project coordination
Laurence Ostyn, nai010 publishers

Graphic design
Christine Alberts, Coppens Alberts

Lithography and Printing
NPN drukkers

Paper
Amber Graphic

Publisher
Marcel Witvoet, nai010 publishers,
Rotterdam

© 2020
nai010 publishers, Rotterdam

nai010 publishers is an internationally
orientated publisher specialized
in developing, producing and
distributing books in the fields of
architecture, urbanism, art and
design. www.nai010.com

nai010 books are available
internationally at selected bookstores
and from the following distribution
partners:

North, Central and South America
– Artbook | D.A.P., New York, USA,
dap@dapinc.com

Rest of the world – Idea Books,
Amsterdam, the Netherlands,
idea@ideabooks.nl

For general questions, please contact
nai010 publishers directly at
sales@nai010.com or visit our
website www.nai010.com for further
information.

Printed and bound the Netherlands

ISBN 978-94-6208-556-5
BISAC ARC005080
NUR 648

Title is also available as e-book:
ISBN ISBN 978-94-6208-566-4
(e-book)

Het Nieuwe Instituut

programme
Landscape & Interior

dossier
Jaap Bakema Study Centre

Total Space explores interdisciplinary exchanges between the fields of architecture, urban planning, anthropology, and systems theory. From the first propositions for networked cities and megastructures in the 1950s and 60s, up to developments such as smart cities and virtual territories today, the concept of a total, all-encompassing space remains a recurrent motif.

project
Total Space

graphic design
Christine Alberts

TUDelft   Delft University of Technology